HAVE FAITH IN MASSACHUSETTS

Coolidge Press is the imprint of the Calvin Coolidge Presidential Foundation, a nonprofit devoted to sharing the life and values of President Calvin Coolidge with all Americans.

The Coolidge Press is publishing a series of collections of Coolidge speeches. Series editors are Amity Shlaes and Matthew Denhart; content and production supervisor is Jed Donahue.

HAVE FAITH IN MASSACHUSETTS

THE REMARKABLE BOOK THAT
INTRODUCED AMERICA TO
CALVIN COOLIDGE

Foreword by
GOVERNOR JAMES H. DOUGLAS

Series Editors
AMITY SHLAES AND MATTHEW DENHART

COOLIDGE
P R E S S
Plymouth Notch, Vermont

Library of Congress Control Number: 2022950903

ISBN: 979-8-9873737-0-5

Published in the United States by
Coolidge Press
The imprint of the Calvin Coolidge Presidential Foundation
Plymouth Notch, Vermont

Manufactured in the United States of America

CONTENTS

FOREWORD TO THE NEW EDITION

BY GOVERNOR JAMES H. DOUGLAS

❦

A book can change history, and the one before your eyes did.

The 1920 Republican National Convention in Chicago marked the origin of the "smoke-filled room." Party leaders behind suite doors at the Blackstone Hotel selected the Republican candidate for president, Senator Warren Gamaliel Harding. The rest of the nine-hundred-odd delegates, waiting at the Chicago Coliseum, resented the secret dealings. By the time the moment came to nominate the vice president, the crowd was spoiling for a chance to humiliate the Old Guard. Delegates blocked the party leaders' choice, Senator Irvine Lenroot of

Wisconsin. Individual delegates began to moot their own candidates for the second spot.

One delegate, Wallace McCamant of Oregon, had recently read a book called *Have Faith in Massachusetts.* The author was the governor of Massachusetts, Calvin Coolidge. McCamant had never met the Bay State governor, who had taken office less than two years earlier. But Coolidge's book had grabbed his attention. "I was impressed with Governor Coolidge's sterling Americanism, his fine spirit during the World War, the soundness of his thinking, and the conservative trend of his thoughts," McCamant later recalled. Without consulting the power brokers, McCamant jumped on a chair and nominated the Massachusetts governor for vice president. Elated at the chance to pick their own man, delegates voted Coolidge onto the ticket. The *Boston Globe* described the effect: "The flames bursting out in every delegation ran round the galleries as if on the wings of a gale." The *Globe* called Coolidge's nomination "the first real, wholly unpremeditated stampede that ever took place at a national convention."

The idea for the book that elevated Coolidge came from the owner of a Boston department store, Frank Stearns. While still a state senator, Coolidge had impressed the proprietor of R. H. Stearns with his integrity and his speeches. Especially strong, Stearns thought, was a speech Coolidge gave when he became president of the Massachusetts senate in 1914: "Have Faith in Massachusetts." With an eye to getting Coolidge onto the national stage one day, Stearns convinced a Boston publishing house, Houghton Mifflin, to collect Coolidge's speeches in a book. In September 1919, just before publication — Stearns was already reviewing page proofs — Governor Coolidge confronted a crisis. The Boston police went on strike, leaving the city's streets unguarded. Riots ensued. Most observers expected Coolidge to compromise with the strikers, as leaders in other cities had done in that time of labor unrest. Yet Governor Coolidge did not compromise. He and the police commissioner fired the policemen. Coolidge declared, "There is no right to strike against the public safety by anybody, anywhere, any time."

Coolidge's categoric statement made headlines across America and resonated with a nation that had grown weary of strikes and violence. The publisher rushed to add to the volume several texts from the strike, printing the package under the title *Have Faith in Massachusetts* well in time for the presidential contest the following year. Stearns also ensured that copies of *Have Faith* reached hundreds of Republican delegates well before they traveled to the Chicago convention. Throughout the 1920 campaign, Harding and Coolidge backers mailed and handed out *Have Faith* to interested voters. For the vice-presidential nominee, "the book was the campaign and the campaign was the book," notes Craig Fehrman, author of a book on presidential writings. The Harding-Coolidge ticket won in a landslide.

This book also helped introduce Coolidge to the American public when he became president after Harding's sudden death in August 1923. "Have Faith in Coolidge," read the headline of an editorial welcoming the nation's new chief executive that was reprinted across the nation, including in the *Wall Street Journal*. The editorial concluded, "No man ever entered the Presidential office better equipped for a policy of action and with less necessity of words." As that editorial observed, newspapers had begun "publishing extracts from his speeches" to inform readers about the new president. For example, the *Los Angeles Times* reprinted Coolidge's 1914 "Have Faith" speech, brashly placing over it the headline "My Policies" and the byline "Calvin Coolidge."

"Have Faith" is an extraordinary speech — one that students at the Calvin Coolidge Presidential Foundation often declaim. In the address, Coolidge offers practical guidance on the operation of government: "Do the day's work. If it be to protect the rights of the weak, whoever objects, do it. If it be to help a powerful corporation better to serve the people, whatever the opposition, do that." As the *Los Angeles Times* recognized, Coolidge's exhortations applied not just to Massachusetts but to the whole nation.

This slim volume, which covers Coolidge's years as a Massachusetts lawmaker, showcases his talent for clear and concise thinking as well as the care he devoted to writing his speeches. As the *New York Times* noted in its review of *Have Faith in Massachusetts*, this book reveals Coolidge's "unusual gift in epigram." You will find a nugget of wisdom for any occasion: "The man who builds a factory builds a temple." "When you deny the right to a profit, you deny the right of a reward to thrift and industry." "Works which endure come from the soul of the people." "The States are the sheet-anchors of our institutions." "The laws of a republic represent its ideals." "Have faith in the moral power of America." Here's one of my favorites: "Man has a spiritual nature. Touch it, and it must respond as the magnet responds to the pole."

Coolidge could also be poetic. He spoke numerous times at Tremont Temple, a Baptist church near the Massachusetts State House. In a speech there in November 1919, he proclaimed, "We must eternally smite the rock of public conscience if the waters of patriotism are to pour forth."

This book shows Coolidge braving confrontation. You'll read in these pages Coolidge's renowned telegram to Samuel Gompers, president of the American Federation of Labor, sent during the Boston police strike. But the same book also shows Coolidge's humanity and decency. Although he disagreed with Gompers on the strike, he appreciated the man's leadership. Just thirteen days before he sent the telegram, Coolidge gave a Labor Day speech in which he admiringly cited Gompers's thoughts: "America may not be perfect. It has the imperfection of all things human. But it is the best country on earth."

Some of the speeches shed light on the important but neglected work of town and state government. You'll read commencement addresses, dedicatory speeches, historical commemorations, and gubernatorial proclamations. As a longtime governor, I came to see the importance of stopping in towns and villages to connect with the people. The work is routine but crucial. In Coolidge's case, these addresses include some profound and memorable quotations. For example, in 1918, on the anniversary of the Battle of Bunker Hill, Lieutenant Governor Coolidge asserted: "The law of progress and civilization is not the law of the jungle.... It does not mean the survival of the fittest, it means the sacrifice of the fittest."

What accounts for the clarity and depth of Coolidge's writing? As a high schooler at Black River Academy and in college at Amherst, Coolidge was educated in the Classics. In college and after, he learned through debate and public speaking. Later, as a clerk, he followed Abraham Lincoln's model and "read law" instead of attending law school. That meant he pored over not only Bay State statutes and the U.S. Constitution but also Blackstone and Coke, the fine texts of the common-law tradition. Years of taking in the cadence and tone of sermons from the pulpits of New England churches schooled him in the power of the shorter address.

Coolidge's rhetorical skill was also informed, I believe, by his upbringing in the hills of Vermont. Coolidge's family and neighbors were laconic, choosing their words with care. Small-town values of patriotism, honesty, and hard work permeated his boyhood in the Vermont hamlet of Plymouth Notch. For the Coolidges, as for many New Englanders, public service was more than a vocation; those who choose to serve "look on it only as an avocation," Coolidge said during his 1915 speech "On the Nature of Politics." Asked once about his hobbies, Coolidge replied that his was "holding office." John Coolidge, Coolidge's father, served as constable, deputy sheriff, selectman, state representative, and state senator. Grandfather Calvin Galusha Coolidge also served in the state legislature. Coolidge absorbed all their wisdom and didn't refrain from giving some of it back. Shortly before Coolidge's father was elected to the Vermont state senate, in 1910, the son, who then served as mayor of Northampton, Massachusetts, advised the parent: "It is much more important to kill bad bills than to pass good ones."

Coolidge was probably the last president who wrote most of his own speeches; indeed, he agonized over them, as his wife, Grace Coolidge, once ruefully attested. But the effort is what makes them so powerful. The Coolidge Foundation plans to publish future volumes of Coolidge speeches. Those volumes will include Coolidge's work as vice president and president.

Don't rush through this book. Take your time; savor each speech. Coolidge crafted these addresses carefully. He was proud of them.

I'm an unabashed fan of our thirtieth president. I hope that, after reading this collection of his thoughts, you will be, too.

James H. Douglas served as governor of Vermont from 2003 to 2011. He is vice chair of the Calvin Coolidge Presidential Foundation.

TIME LINE

∽

July 4, 1872	John Calvin Coolidge is born to John Coolidge and Victoria Moor Coolidge in Plymouth Notch, Vermont. In 1875, a sister, Abigail Gratia (Abbie) Coolidge, is born.
March 14, 1885	Calvin's mother, Victoria, dies.
1886–1890	Coolidge attends boarding school at Black River Academy in Ludlow, Vermont.
March 6, 1890	Calvin's sister, Abbie, dies at age fourteen, probably of appendicitis.
Autumn 1891	Coolidge enrolls in Amherst College, graduating cum laude in 1895. Though shy, he makes a name for himself on campus as a debater.

September 1895   The Coolidge family decides against law school.
                  Coolidge will "read law," an old common-law
                  country practice of learning at a firm, at Ham-
                  mond and Field in Northampton, Massachu-
                  setts. He drops "John" from his name, becom-
                  ing simply "Calvin Coolidge."

1897–1904   Coolidge begins his climb in Bay State law and
                  politics, opening his own law practice and serv-
                  ing in various local political positions, includ-
                  ing Republican city ward committeeman, city
                  councilman, city solicitor, clerk of courts of
                  Hampshire County, and Republican city com-
                  mittee chairman for Northampton.

October 4, 1905   Coolidge marries Grace Anna Goodhue, a
                  trainee at the Clarke School for the Deaf. The
                  Coolidges rent half of a two-family home at
                  21 Massasoit Street in Northampton.

September 7, 1906 A son, John Coolidge, is born to Calvin and
                  Grace.

1906–1909   Coolidge is elected to and serves two terms in
                  the Massachusetts House of Representatives.

April 13, 1908   A second son, Calvin Coolidge Jr., is born to
                  Calvin and Grace.

1909–1911   Coolidge is elected mayor of Northampton and
                  serves two terms.

1911–1915   Coolidge is elected to and serves multiple
                  terms in the Massachusetts senate. An impor-

tant mentor is U.S. senator W. Murray Crane, who leads the famous paper company Crane's.

February 3, 1913   The Sixteenth Amendment to the U.S. Constitution is ratified, establishing Congress's right to impose a federal income tax.

April 8, 1913   The Seventeenth Amendment to the U.S. Constitution is ratified, allowing voters to cast direct votes for U.S. senators rather than having state legislatures choose a state's representatives to the U.S. Senate.

January 7, 1914   Calvin Coolidge delivers the speech "Have Faith in Massachusetts" on becoming president of the state senate. The address establishes Coolidge as an important figure in Massachusetts and even draws attention outside the state.

1915–1918   Coolidge is elected lieutenant governor of Massachusetts and serves two terms.

April 6, 1917   The United States ends its neutral stance in World War I by declaring war on Germany.

November 5, 1918   Coolidge is elected governor of Massachusetts at age forty-six.

November 11, 1918   Armistice Day marks the end of World War I.

January 16, 1919   The Eighteenth Amendment to the U.S. Constitution is ratified, establishing the prohibition of alcohol in the United States.

June 4, 1919   The Nineteenth Amendment to the U.S. Con-
                      stitution is ratified, granting women the right
                      to vote.

September 3, 1919   Governor Coolidge delivers a speech celebrat-
                      ing the 250th anniversary of Westfield, Massa-
                      chusetts. He highlights the importance of the
                      U.S. Constitution as a unifying document.

September 1919   The Boston police force breaks its contract and
                      goes on strike to protest low wages and poor
                      conditions. Governor Coolidge takes strong
                      action to ensure law and order. Coolidge calls
                      out the Massachusetts State Guard and fires
                      the policemen. Coolidge's handling of the cri-
                      sis catapults him to national prominence.

October 1919   *Have Faith in Massachusetts* is first published.
                      The book earns attention from such promi-
                      nent publications as the *New York Times*,
                      the *Wall Street Journal*, and the *Los Ange-
                      les Times*. The publisher, Houghton Mifflin,
                      will ultimately distribute some seventy-three
                      thousand copies of *Have Faith in Massachu-
                      setts* — nearly a quarter million copies when
                      adjusted for today's population.

November 1919   Coolidge is reelected governor of Massachusetts.

June 12, 1920   With the United States mired in debt from
                      World War I, burdened by high taxes, and vying
                      with Britain to become the world's leading eco-
                      nomic power, the Republican National Conven-
                      tion nominates candidates for president and vice

president who emphasize economic programs to sustain prosperity: Warren Harding and Calvin Coolidge, respectively. The Harding-Coolidge campaign runs with the promise of less uncertain business conditions, lower taxes, budgetary rigor, and "a return to normalcy."

November 2, 1920   Harding is elected president of the United States; Coolidge is elected vice president. The Coolidges move to Washington, D.C., and take up residence in the New Willard Hotel.

June 10, 1921   The Budget and Accounting Act of 1921 gives the president his own research staff, via the new Bureau of the Budget, and wider authority to manage the federal budget. The new tools make it easier for Presidents Harding and Coolidge to restrain congressional spending.

August 10, 1922   Vice President Coolidge delivers the speech "Limitations of the Law" in San Francisco. Coolidge says, "There is no justification for public interference with purely private concerns."

August 3, 1923   News of President Harding's death reaches the Coolidges while they vacation in Plymouth Notch. Coolidge is sworn in as president by his father, John Coolidge, a notary public. The humility displayed in this event becomes a hallmark of the Coolidge presidency.

1924   Sales of a new apparatus, the radio, exceed $350 million, an exponential increase from the level at the start of the decade.

May 15, 1924   Coolidge vetoes a bill to give bonuses to veter-
                    ans of World War I, fearing that the bonuses
                    will overstretch the budget. In his veto mes-
                    sage, Coolidge writes, "The gratitude of the
                    Nation to these veterans can not be expressed
                    in dollars and cents." He continues: "Patriotism
                    can neither be bought nor sold. It is not hire
                    and salary. It is not material, but spiritual."
                    Congress later overrides Coolidge's veto.

May 24, 1924   With overwhelming bipartisan support, Con-
                    gress passes the Johnson-Reed Immigration
                    Act, halting most immigration from eastern
                    and southern Europe, as well as from Japan.
                    Coolidge signs the bill into law, noting his
                    regret over, in particular, the Japanese exclu-
                    sion provision, which he calls "deplorable."

June 2, 1924   Coolidge signs legislation cutting tax rates and
                    promises to "bend his energies" for further cuts.

June 2, 1924   Coolidge signs the Indian Citizenship Act,
                    which declares that "all non-citizen Indians
                    born within the territorial limits of the United
                    States be, and they are hereby, declared to be
                    citizens of the United States."

June 6, 1924   Coolidge delivers the commencement speech
                    at Howard University, a historically black col-
                    lege in Washington, D.C.

July 7, 1924   Coolidge's younger son, Calvin Jr., dies of sep-
                    sis from a blister he sustained while playing
                    tennis on the White House court.

October 26, 1924   Coolidge delivers his "Discriminating Benevo-
                    lence" speech over the phone from the White
                    House to an audience of the Federation of Jew-
                    ish Philanthropic Societies of New York City,
                    remarking, "I regard a good budget as among
                    the noblest monuments of virtue." He com-
                    mends the community leaders, telling them, "I
                    want you to know that I feel you are making
                    good citizens, that you are strengthening the
                    government, that you are demonstrating the
                    supremacy of the spiritual life and helping
                    establish the Kingdom of God on earth."

November 4, 1924   Coolidge is elected president in a landslide,
                    earning an absolute majority of the popu-
                    lar vote in a three-way race with Democrat
                    John W. Davis and Progressive Party candidate
                    Robert La Follette.

November 1924   Macy's holds its first Thanksgiving Day Parade.

1925   Sears, Roebuck opens its first direct retail store,
                    expanding to more than 300 stores nation-
                    wide by the end of the decade. Chain stores
                    spring up widely during the 1920s as consum-
                    ers become more confident in the prosperous
                    economy.

October 6, 1925   In Omaha, Nebraska, Coolidge delivers the
                    speech "Toleration and Liberalism," a call for
                    unity among all citizens, whatever their ethnic
                    background. Coolidge says: "Whether one
                    traces his Americanism back three centuries to
                    the *Mayflower*, or three years to the steerage,

is not half so important as whether his Americanism of today is real and genuine. No matter by what various crafts we came here, we are all now in the same boat."

February 1926   President Coolidge signs the Revenue Act of 1926, decreasing the top marginal income tax rate to 25 percent.

March 18, 1926   Coolidge's father, Colonel John Coolidge, dies in Plymouth Notch.

May 1926   A general strike paralyzes British industry and political life after mine owners threaten to cut pay and increase hours. Troubled Britain increasingly provides a contrast to the United States, where productivity gains are strong enough that industry is shifting from the traditional six-day workweek to a new five-day-a-week model, with paid vacations becoming more common. American economic primacy is solidifying.

July 5, 1926   Coolidge delivers "The Inspiration of the Declaration" speech in Philadelphia to celebrate the 150th anniversary of the signing of the Declaration of Independence. He asserts: "If all men are created equal, that is final. If they are endowed with inalienable rights, that is final. If governments derive their just powers from the consent of the governed, that is final. No advance, no progress can be made beyond these propositions."

February 25, 1927   Coolidge vetoes the McNary-Haugen Farm
                     Relief Act, by which the federal government
                     would fix agricultural prices and then buy farm-
                     ers' products at those artificially high prices.

Spring 1927   The Mississippi River floods to unprecedented
                     levels, displacing hundreds of thousands of
                     people in Mississippi, Arkansas, and Louisiana.
                     Like President Grover Cleveland before him,
                     Coolidge refrains from traveling to flood sites,
                     wary of setting a precedent of large-scale fed-
                     eral rescues during natural disasters.

August 2, 1927   Coolidge announces, "I do not choose to run
                     for President in nineteen twenty eight," via
                     handwritten slips of paper given to reporters
                     in Rapid City, South Dakota, the site of the
                     1927 Summer White House.

October 20, 1927   The Ford Model A comes to market, the sec-
                     ond mass model produced by the Ford Motor
                     Company. The previous Model T automobile
                     was available for eighteen years.

November 1927   Flooding in Coolidge's own Vermont causes
                     damage and destruction throughout the state.
                     As he did earlier in the year after the Missis-
                     sippi flood, the president stays away from the
                     disaster site and pursues a restrained federal
                     response.

May 23, 1928   Coolidge vetoes the McNary-Haugen Act for a
                     second time.

May 26, 1928   Coolidge is presented with a bill to use fed-
                        eral resources to dam the Tennessee River to
                        generate energy. The president uses the pocket
                        veto to block the bill.

September 21, 1928   Coolidge delivers a brief speech at Benning-
                        ton, fondly proclaiming, "Vermont is a state I
                        love." The speech follows two days of touring
                        the Green Mountain State to see the progress
                        of recovery efforts after the previous year's
                        devastating flood.

November 6, 1928   Coolidge's secretary of commerce, Herbert
                        Hoover, is elected president of the United
                        States.

January 17, 1929   Coolidge signs the Kellogg-Briand Pact into
                        law. Under the treaty, sixty-two nations agree
                        to renounce war as a means of international
                        policy.

March 4, 1929   Coolidge leaves office, having balanced the
                        federal budget every year while president.
                        Coolidge's budget efforts have resulted in a
                        significant reduction in the size of the national
                        debt and a decrease in overall federal spend-
                        ing. The national debt falls by a third during
                        the Coolidge presidency, from $22.3 billion in
                        1923 to $16.9 billion in 1929. The Coolidges
                        return via rail to Northampton.

May 1929   *The Autobiography of Calvin Coolidge* is first
                        published.

Autumn 1929 The stock market crashes.

1930 The Coolidges move to a more private home in Northampton, the Beeches.

June 1930–June 1931 Coolidge writes a syndicated daily newspaper column, "Calvin Coolidge Says."

1932 Unemployment rises past 20 percent. New York governor Franklin Delano Roosevelt is elected U.S. president. Roosevelt's "New Deal" promises active government and progressivism.

January 5, 1933 Coolidge dies at age sixty at the Beeches. The *Wall Street Journal* comments that although the New Deal might undo some of Coolidge's achievements, "in due time, the good fortune of the United States to have had such a man as Calvin Coolidge in just the years he filled that office will be more clearly realized than it has yet been."

September 16, 1956 The Forbes Library in Northampton, which possesses many of the papers and other ephemera related to Calvin Coolidge, dedicates the Calvin Coolidge Memorial Room.

July 8, 1957 Former first lady Grace Coolidge dies at age seventy-eight.

1960 President Coolidge's son John Coolidge and a group of friends and supporters found the Coolidge Foundation to preserve the legacy of Coolidge's time in office. The Foundation begins a long partnership with the state of Vermont at the historic birthplace site in Plymouth Notch.

1981   President Ronald Reagan places a portrait of Coolidge in the White House Cabinet Room.

May 31, 2000   Coolidge's elder son, John Coolidge, dies at age ninety-three.

HAVE FAITH IN
MASSACHUSETTS

NOTE TO READER:
This edition of *Have Faith in Massachusetts* preserves
the spelling and punctuation that appeared in the first
edition, which Houghton Mifflin published in 1919.

INTRODUCTORY NOTE

◦◦◦

Calvin Coolidge's biggest supporter, the merchant Frank W. Stearns, convinced Boston publisher Houghton Mifflin to release this book. The timing of publication proved fortuitous: Houghton Mifflin sent Have Faith in Massachusetts *to press in September 1919, right after Governor Coolidge's decisive action in the Boston police strike made him a national figure. Houghton Mifflin editor Roger Scaife probably wrote this introductory note.*

There are certain fundamental principles of sound community life which cannot be stated too emphatically or too often. Few public men of to-day have shown a finer combination of right feeling and clear thinking

3

about these principles, with a gift for the pithy expression of them, than has Governor Calvin Coolidge. It was an accurate phrase that President Meiklejohn* used when, in conferring the degree of Doctor of Laws on him at Amherst College last June, he complimented him on teaching the lesson of "adequate brevity."

His speeches and messages abound in evidences of this gift, but in the main the speeches are not easily accessible. It has seemed to some of Governor Coolidge's admirers,† as it has to the publishers of this little volume, that a real public service might be rendered by making a careful selection from the best of the speeches and issuing them in an attractive and convenient form. With his permission this has been done,‡ and it is hoped that many readers will welcome the book in this time of special need of inspiring and steadying influences.

It is a time when all men should realize that, in the words of Governor Coolidge himself, "Laws must rest on the eternal foundations of righteousness"; that "Industry,

---

* Alexander Meiklejohn served as president of Amherst College, Coolidge's alma mater, from 1913 to 1924.

† Coolidge's most ardent admirer was Frank W. Stearns, a fellow Amherst alumnus. Stearns, the owner of the department store R. H. Stearns, saw Coolidge as an ambassador for civilization in rough times. Stearns invested thousands of dollars in advertising *Have Faith in Massachusetts* and handed out copies all over the country. Craig Fehrman, in his book *Author in Chief*, reports that Stearns ultimately distributed seventy-three thousand copies, which equates to nearly a quarter million copies when adjusted for today's population.

‡ When Stearns approached Coolidge about the book idea, the governor responded, "All right, but I'll have nothing to do with it."

thrift, character are not conferred by act or resolve. Government cannot relieve from toil." It is a time when we must "have faith in Massachusetts. We need a broader, firmer, deeper faith in the people, — a faith that men desire to do right, that the Commonwealth is founded upon a righteousness which will endure."

THE EDITORS

Boston, September, 1919

I

TO THE STATE SENATE ON
BEING ELECTED ITS PRESIDENT

JANUARY 7, 1914

"Men do not make laws. They do but discover them."

This speech, from which this volume derives its title, established Coolidge as an important figure in Massachusetts. It also drew notice outside the state. Former president William Howard Taft wrote, "It strikes a chord in my heart that responds to every word." Coolidge later remarked, "The effect was beyond my expectation." The address offers insight into Coolidge's political philosophy, including his views on federalism, representative democracy, rights, the limitations of government, and the spiritual foundations of liberty.

Honorable Senators: — I thank you — with gratitude for the high honor given, with appreciation for the solemn obligations assumed — I thank you.

This Commonwealth is one. We are all members of one body. The welfare of the weakest and the welfare of the most powerful are inseparably bound together. Industry cannot flourish if labor languish. Transportation cannot prosper if manufactures decline. The general welfare cannot be provided for in any one act, but it is well to remember that the benefit of one is the benefit of all, and the neglect of one is the neglect of all. The suspension of one man's dividends is the suspension of another man's pay envelope.

Men do not make laws. They do but discover them. Laws must be justified by something more than the will of the majority. They must rest on the eternal foundation of righteousness. That state is most fortunate in its form of government which has the aptest instruments for the discovery of laws. The latest, most modern, and nearest perfect system that statesmanship has devised is representative government. Its weakness is the weakness of us imperfect human beings who administer it. Its strength is that even such administration secures to the people more blessings than any other system ever produced. No nation has discarded it and retained liberty. Representative government must be preserved.

Courts are established, not to determine the popularity of a cause, but to adjudicate and enforce rights. No litigant should be required to submit his case to the hazard and expense of a political campaign. No judge should be required to seek or receive political rewards. The courts of Massachusetts are known and honored wherever men love justice. Let their glory suffer no diminution at our hands. The electorate and judiciary cannot combine. A hearing means a hearing. When the trial of causes goes outside the court-room, Anglo-Saxon constitutional government ends.

The people cannot look to legislation generally for success. Industry, thrift, character are not conferred by act or resolve. Government cannot relieve from toil. It can provide no substitute for the rewards of service. It can, of course, care for the defective and recognize distinguished merit. The normal must care for themselves. Self-government means self-support.

Man is born into the universe with a personality that is his own. He has a right that is founded upon the constitution of the universe to have property that is his own. Ultimately, property rights and personal rights are the same thing. The one cannot be preserved if the other be violated. Each man is entitled to his rights and the rewards of his service be they never so large or never so small.

History reveals no civilized people among whom there were not a highly educated class, and large aggregations of wealth, represented usually by the clergy and the nobility. Inspiration has always come from above. Diffusion of learning has come down from the university to the common school — the kindergarten is last. No one would now expect to aid the common school by abolishing higher education.

It may be that the diffusion of wealth works in an analogous way. As the little red schoolhouse is builded in the college, it may be that the fostering and protection of large aggregations of wealth are the only foundation on which to build the prosperity of the whole people. Large profits mean large pay rolls. But profits must be the result of service performed. In no land are there so many and such large aggregations of wealth as here; in no land do they perform larger service; in no land will the work of a day bring so large a reward in material and spiritual welfare.

Have faith in Massachusetts. In some unimportant detail some other States may surpass her, but in the general results, there is no place on earth where the people secure, in a larger measure, the blessings of organized government, and nowhere can those functions more properly be termed self-government.

Do the day's work. If it be to protect the rights of the weak, whoever objects, do it. If it be to help a powerful corporation better to serve the people, whatever the opposition, do that. Expect to be called a stand-patter, but don't be a stand-patter. Expect to be called a demagogue, but don't be a demagogue. Don't hesitate to be as revolutionary as science. Don't hesitate to be as reactionary as the multiplication table. Don't expect to build up the weak by pulling down the strong. Don't hurry to legislate. Give administration a chance to catch up with legislation.

We need a broader, firmer, deeper faith in the people — a faith that men desire to do right, that the Commonwealth is founded upon a righteousness which will endure, a reconstructed faith that the final approval of the people is given not to demagogues, slavishly pandering to their selfishness, merchandising with the clamor of the hour, but to statesmen, ministering to their welfare, representing their deep, silent, abiding convictions.

Statutes must appeal to more than material welfare. Wages won't satisfy, be they never so large. Nor houses; nor lands; nor coupons, though they fall thick as the leaves of autumn. Man has a spiritual nature. Touch it, and it must respond as the magnet responds to the pole. To that, not to selfishness, let the laws of the Commonwealth appeal. Recognize the immortal worth and dignity of man. Let the laws of Massachusetts proclaim to her humblest citizen, performing the most menial task, the recognition of his manhood, the recognition that all men are peers, the humblest with the most exalted, the recognition that all work is glorified. Such is the path to equality before the law. Such is the foundation of liberty under the law. Such is the sublime revelation of man's relation to man — Democracy.

II

AMHERST COLLEGE
ALUMNI ASSOCIATION,
BOSTON

FEBRUARY 4, 1916

"Work is not a curse, it is the prerogative
of intelligence, the only means to manhood,
and the measure of civilization."

*Coolidge graduated from Amherst College in 1895. Twenty-
one years later, the college celebrated his rise to lieutenant
governor of Massachusetts. More than a thousand people,
including alumni and the entire Amherst faculty, attended a
grand dinner at Boston's Copley Plaza. Coolidge pressed his
fellow alumni to stay true to the college's doctrine of striv-
ing to create and to work.*

We live in an age which questions everything.
The past generation was one of religious criticism. This is one of commercial criticism.

We have seen the development of great industries. It
has been represented that some of these have not been

free from blame. In this development some men have seemed to prosper beyond the measure of their service, while others have appeared to be bound to toil beyond their strength for less than a decent livelihood.

As a result of criticising these conditions there has grown up a too well-developed public opinion along two lines; one, that the men engaged in great affairs are selfish and greedy and not to be trusted, that business activity is not moral and the whole system is to be condemned; and the other, that employment, that work, is a curse to man, and that working hours ought to be as short as possible or in some way abolished. After criticism, our religious faith emerged clearer and stronger and freed from doubt. So will our business relations emerge, purified but justified.

The evidence of evolution and the facts of history tell us of the progress and development of man through various steps and ages, known by various names. We learn of the stone age, the bronze, and the iron age. We can see the different steps in the growth of the forms of government; how anarchy was put down by the strong arm of the despot, of the growth of aristocracy, of limited monarchies and of parliaments, and finally democracy.

But in all these changes man took but one step at a time. Where we can trace history, no race ever stepped directly from the stone age to the iron age and no nation ever passed directly from despotism to democracy. Each advance has been made only when a previous stage was approaching perfection, even to conditions which are now sometimes lost arts.

We have reached the age of invention, of commerce, of great industrial enterprise. It is often referred to as selfish and materialistic.

Our economic system has been attacked from above and from below. But the short answer lies in the teachings of history. The hope of a Watt or an Edison lay in the men who chipped flint to perfection.* The seed of democracy lay in a perfected despotism. The hope of to-morrow lies in the development of the instruments of to-day. The prospect of advance lies in maintaining those conditions which have stimulated invention and industry and commerce. The only road to a more progressive age lies in perfecting the instrumentalities of this age.

The only hope for peace lies in the perfection of the arts of war.

"We build the ladder by which we rise

. . .

And we mount to the summit round by round."†

---

* Here Coolidge refers to the inventors James Watt (best known for improving the steam engine) and Thomas Edison (who held more than a thousand patents).

† From the poem "Gradatim" by the nineteenth-century poet and novelist Josiah Gilbert Holland. The full stanza reads: "Heaven is not reached at a single bound; / But we build the ladder by which we rise / From the lowly earth to the vaulted skies, / And we mount to its summit round by round."

All growth depends upon activity. Life is manifest only by action. There is no development physically or intellectually without effort, and effort means work. Work is not a curse, it is the prerogative of intelligence, the only means to manhood, and the measure of civilization. Savages do not work. The growth of a sentiment that despises work is an appeal from civilization to barbarism.

I would not be understood as making a sweeping criticism of current legislation along these lines. I, too, rejoice that an awakened conscience has outlawed commercial standards that were false or low and that an awakened humanity has decreed that the working and living condition of our citizens must be worthy of true manhood and true womanhood.

I agree that the measure of success is not merchandise but character. But I do criticise those sentiments, held in all too respectable quarters, that our economic system is fundamentally wrong, that commerce is only selfishness, and that our citizens, holding the hope of all that America means, are living in industrial slavery. I appeal to Amherst men to reiterate and sustain the Amherst doctrine, that the man who builds a factory builds a temple, that the man who works there worships there, and to each is due, not scorn and blame, but reverence and praise.

III

BROCKTON CHAMBER
OF COMMERCE

APRIL 11, 1916

"Where wealth has accumulated, there the arts and
sciences have flourished, there education has been
diffused, and of contemplation liberty has been born."

*The enduring caricature of Coolidge portrays him as a tool of
big business, concerned with material success alone. Yet here
Coolidge cautions critics not to mistake "the means for the
end." Commerce, he says, "is the foundation of human progress and prosperity and the great artisan of human character."*

M an's nature drives him ever onward. He is forever
seeking development. At one time it may be by
the chase, at another by warfare, and again by the quiet
arts of peace and commerce, but something within is ever
calling him on to "replenish the earth and subdue it."*

---

* Genesis 1:28.

17

It may be of little importance to determine at any time just where we are, but it is of the utmost importance to determine whither we are going. Set the course aright and time must bring mankind to the ultimate goal.

We are living in a commercial age. It is often designated as selfish and materialistic. We are told that everything has been commercialized. They say it has not been enough that this spirit should dominate the marts of trade, it has spread to every avenue of human endeavor, to our arts, our sciences and professions, our politics, our educational institutions and even into the pulpit; and because of this there are those who have gone so far in their criticism of commercialism as to advocate the destruction of all enterprise and the abolition of all property.

Destructive criticism is always easy because, despite some campaign oratory, some of us are not yet perfect. But constructive criticism is not so easy. The faults of commercialism, like many other faults, lie in the use we make of it. Before we decide upon a wholesale condemnation of the most noteworthy spirit of modern times it would be well to examine carefully what that spirit has done to advance the welfare of mankind.

Wherever we can read human history, the answer is always the same. Where commerce has flourished there civilization has increased. It has not sufficed that men should tend their flocks, and maintain themselves in comfort on their industry alone, however great. It is only when the exchange of products begins that development follows. This was the case in ancient Babylon, whose records of trade and banking we are just beginning to read. Their merchandise went by canal and caravan to the ends of the earth. It was not the war galleys, but the merchant vessels of Phoenicia, of Tyre, and Carthage that brought them civilization and power. To-day it is not the battle fleet, but the mercantile marine which in the end will determine the destiny of nations. The advance of our own land has been due to our trade, and the comfort and happiness of our people are dependent on our general business conditions. It is only a figure of poetry that "wealth accumulates and men decay."* Where wealth has accumulated, there the arts and sciences have flourished, there education has been diffused, and of contemplation liberty has been born. The progress of man has been measured by his commercial prosperity. I believe that these considerations are sufficient to justify our business enterprise and activity, but there are still deeper reasons.

I have intended to indicate not only that commerce is an instrument of great power, but that commercial development is necessary to all human progress. What, then, of the prevalent criticism? Men have mistaken the means for the end. It is not enough for the individual

---

* This line originated with Oliver Goldsmith, in his 1770 poem "The Deserted Village," which blames greedy landowners for destroying agrarian villagers' way of life. Later, in the 1928 book *The Intelligent Woman's Guide to Socialism and Capitalism*, the Irish playwright and polemicist George Bernard Shaw would title an essay "How Wealth Accumulates and Men Decay."

or the nation to acquire riches. Money will not purchase character or good government. We are under the injunction to "replenish the earth and subdue it," not so much because of the help a new earth will be to us, as because by that process man is to find himself and thereby realize his highest destiny. Men must work for more than wages, factories must turn out more than merchandise, or there is naught but black despair ahead.

If material rewards be the only measure of success, there is no hope of a peaceful solution of our social questions, for they will never be large enough to satisfy. But such is not the case. Men struggle for material success because that is the path, the process, to the development of character. We ought to demand economic justice but most of all because it is justice. We must forever realize that material rewards are limited and in a sense they are only incidental, but the development of character is unlimited and is the only essential. The measure of success is not the quantity of merchandise, but the quality of manhood which is produced.

These, then, are the justifying conceptions of the spirit of our age; that commerce is the foundation of human progress and prosperity and the great artisan of human character. Let us dismiss the general indictment that has all too long hung over business enterprise. While we continue to condemn, unsparingly, selfishness and greed and all trafficking in the natural rights of man, let us not forget to respect thrift and industry and enterprise. Let us look to the service rather than to the reward. Then shall we see in our industrial army, from the most exalted captain to the humblest soldier in the ranks, a purpose worthy to minister to the highest needs of man and to fulfil the hope of a fairer day.

IV

AT THE HOME OF
DANIEL WEBSTER, MARSHFIELD

JULY 4, 1916

"Above all, the call to duty, the pledge of
fortune and of life, nobility of character through
nobility of action: this is Americanism."

*Coolidge was born on the Fourth of July, and Independence
Day prompted him to reflect on America's meaning. For
example, he gave thoughtful remarks in 1918 (see page 117)
and in 1926. In this 1916 speech, he says the words of the
Declaration of Independence represent a call to action — a
call to live up to the Declaration's "eternal principles."*

History is revelation. It is the manifestation in human
affairs of a "power not ourselves that makes for
righteousness."* Savages have no history. It is the mark

---

* Here Coolidge cites Matthew Arnold's definition of God. The great
critic and poet of Victorian England wrote of God as "an enduring Power, not
ourselves, that makes for righteousness."

of civilization. This New England of ours slumbered from the dawn of creation until the beginning of the seventeenth century, not unpeopled, but with no record of human events worthy of a name. Different races came, and lived, and vanished, but the story of their existence has little more of interest for us than the story the naturalist tells of the animal kingdom, or the geologist relates of the formation of the crust of the earth.* It takes men of larger vision and higher inspiration, with a power to impart a larger vision and a higher inspiration to the people, to make history. It is not a negative, but a positive achievement. It is unconcerned with idolatry or despotism or treason or rebellion or betrayal, but bows in reverence before Moses or Hampden or Washington or Lincoln or the Light that shone on Calvary.†

July 4, 1776, was a day of history in its high and true significance. Not because the underlying principles set out in the Declaration of Independence were new; they

---

* Only eight years after making this comment, President Coolidge signed legislation making all Native Americans citizens of the United States. He hosted Native Americans at the White House many times. In 1927, the Sioux tribe honored Coolidge with the title "Chief Leading Eagle." In his autobiography, Coolidge claimed that his father's family "showed a marked trace of Indian blood."

† Coolidge was both a student and a defender of the Western tradition. In his autobiography, he recalled when he first "learned of the glory and grandeur of the ancient civilization that grew up around the Mediterranean and in Mesopotamia." In this line, "Hampden" refers to John Hampden, the seventeenth-century English figure whose principled opposition to arbitrary taxation made him a model for many American Founders.

are older than the Christian religion, or Greek philosophy, nor was it because history is made by proclamation
or declaration; history is made only by action. But it was
an historic day because the representatives of three millions of people there vocalized Concord and Lexington
and Bunker Hill, which gave notice to the world that
they were acting, and proposed to act, and to found an
independent nation, on the theory that "all men are created equal; that they are endowed by their Creator with
certain inalienable* rights; that among these are life, liberty, and the pursuit of happiness." The wonder and glory
of the American people is not the ringing declaration of
that day, but the action, then already begun, and in the
process of being carried out in spite of every obstacle
that war could interpose, making the theory of freedom
and equality a reality. We revere that day because it
marks the beginnings of independence, the beginnings
of a constitution that was finally to give universal freedom and equality to all American citizens, the beginnings of a government that was to recognize beyond all
others the power and worth and dignity of man. There
began the first of governments to acknowledge that it
was founded on the sovereignty of the people. There the
world first beheld the revelation of modern democracy.

Democracy is not a tearing-down; it is a building-up. It
is not a denial of the divine right of kings; it supplements

---

* The Declaration uses "unalienable" rather than "inalienable."

that claim with the assertion of the divine right of all men. It does not destroy; it fulfils. It is the consummation of all theories of government, to the spirit of which all the nations of the earth must yield. It is the great constructive force of the ages. It is the alpha and omega of man's relation to man, the beginning and the end. There is and can be no more doubt of the triumph of democracy in human affairs, than there is of the triumph of gravitation in the physical world; the only question is how and when. Its foundation lays hold upon eternity.

These are some of the ideals that the founders of our institutions expressed, in part unconsciously, on that momentous day now passed by one hundred and forty years. They knew that ideals do not maintain themselves. They knew that they there declared a purpose which would be resisted by the forces, on land and sea, of the mightiest empire of the earth. Without the resolution of the people of the Colonies to resort to arms, and without the guiding military genius of Washington, the Declaration of Independence would be naught in history but the vision of doctrinaires, a mockery of sounding brass and tinkling cymbal. Let us never forget that it was that resolution and that genius which made it the vitalizing force of a great nation. It takes service and sacrifice to maintain ideals.

But it is far more than the Declaration of Independence that brings us here to-day. That was, indeed, a great document. It was drawn up by Thomas Jefferson

when he was at his best. It was the product of men who
seemed inspired. No greater company ever assembled to
interpret the voice of the people or direct the destinies
of a nation. The events of history may have added to
it, but subtracted nothing. Wisdom and experience have
increased the admiration of it. Time and criticism have
not shaken it. It stands with ordinance and law, char-
ter and constitution, prophecy and revelation, whether
we read them in the history of Babylon, the results of
Runnymede, the Ten Commandments, or the Sermon on
the Mount. But, however worthy of our reverence and
admiration, however preëminent, it was only one incident of a great forward movement of the human race, of
which the American Revolution was itself only a larger
incident. It was not so much a struggle of the Colonies
against the tyranny of bad government, as against wrong
principles of government, and for self-government. It was
man realizing himself. It was sovereignty from within
which responded to the alarm of Paul Revere on that
April night, and which went marching, gun in hand,
against sovereignty from without, wherever it was found
on earth. It only paused at Concord, or Yorktown, then
marched on to Paris, to London, to Moscow, to Pekin.*
Against it the powers of privilege and the forces of

---

* With "Moscow," Coolidge refers to the 1905 Russian Revolution, which
prompted the czar to institute political reforms. Of course, Russia would endure
revolution again a year after Coolidge spoke. "Pekin" was a then-common
romanized name for Beijing.

despotism could not prevail. Superstition and sham cannot stand before intelligence and reality. The light that first broke over the thirteen Colonies lying along the Atlantic Coast was destined to illuminate the world. It has been a struggle against the forces of darkness; victory has been and is still delayed in some quarters, but the result is not in doubt. All the forces of the universe are ranged on the side of democracy. It must prevail.

In the train of this idea there has come to man a long line of collateral blessings. Freedom has many sides and angles. Human slavery has been swept away. With security of personal rights has come security of property rights. The freedom of the human mind is recognized in the right of free speech and free press. The public schools have made education possible for all, and ignorance a disgrace. A most significant development of respect for man has come to be respect for his occupation. It is not alone for the learned professions that great treasures are now poured out. Technical, trade, and vocational schools for teaching skill in occupations are fostered and nourished, with the same care as colleges and universities for the teaching of sciences and the classics. Democracy not only ennobled man; it has ennobled industry. In political affairs the vote of the humblest has long counted for as much as the vote of the most exalted. We are working towards the day when, in our industrial life, equal honor shall fall to equal endeavor, whether it be exhibited in the office or in the shop.

These are some of the results of that great world movement, which, first exhibiting itself in the Continental Congress of America, carried her arms to victory, through the sacrifice of a seven years' revolutionary war, and wrote into the Treaty of Paris the recognition of the right of the people to rule: since which days existence on this planet has had a new meaning; a result which, changing the old order of things, putting the race under the control and guidance of new forces, rescued man from every thraldom, but laid on him every duty.

We know that only ignorance and superstition seek to explain events by fate and destiny, yet there is a fascination in such speculations born, perhaps, of human frailty. How happens it that James Otis laid out in 1762 the then almost treasonable proposition that "Kings were made for the good of the people, and not the people for them," in a pamphlet which was circulated among the Colonists?* What school had taught Patrick Henry that national outlook which he expressed in the opening debates of the first Continental Congress when he said, "I am not a Virginian, but an American," and which hurried him on to the later cry of "Liberty or

---

* James Otis is often credited with the phrase "taxation without representation is tyranny." The Massachusetts lawyer and legislator laid out the principles of that argument in a 1762 pamphlet. He recounted how the royal governor of Massachusetts had authorized expenditures without the consent of the Massachusetts legislature. Otis wrote, "Kings were (and plantation governors should be) made for the good of the people, and not the people for them."

death"? How was it that the filling of a vacancy sent Thomas Jefferson to the second Continental Congress, there to pen the immortal Declaration we this day celebrate? No other living man could have excelled him in preparation for, or in the execution of, that great task. What circumstance put the young George Washington under the military instruction of a former army officer, and then gave him years of training to lead the Continental forces? What settled Ethan Allen in the wilderness of the Green Mountains ready to strike Ticonderoga? Whence came that power to draft state papers, in a new and unlettered land, which compelled the admiration of the cultured Earl of Chatham?* What lengthened out the days of Benjamin Franklin that he might negotiate the Treaty of Paris? What influence sent the miraculous voice of Daniel Webster from the outlying settlements of New Hampshire to rouse the land with his appeal for Liberty and Union?† And finally who raised up Lincoln, to lead, to inspire, and to die, that the opening assertion of the Declaration might stand at last fulfilled?

These thoughts are overpowering. But let us beware of fate and destiny. Barbarians have decreased, but bar-

---

* William Pitt the Elder, 1st Earl of Chatham, emerged as a prominent defender of the American colonies against Britain's increasingly harsh policies. Historian Clinton Rossiter called the British statesman the "idol of the colonies."

† In January 1830, in a famous Senate oration, Daniel Webster of Massachusetts declared, "Liberty and Union, now and forever, one and inseparable!"

barism still exists. Rome boasted the name of the Eternal City. It was but eight hundred years from the sack of the city by one tribe of barbarians to the sack of the city by another tribe of barbarians. Between lay something akin to a democratic commonwealth. Then games, and bribes for the populace, with dictators and Caesars, while later the Praetorian Guard sold the royal purple to the highest bidder. After which came Alaric, the Goth, and night.* Since when democracy lay dormant for some fifteen centuries. We may claim with reason that our Nation has had the guidance of Providence; we may know that our form of government must ultimately prevail upon earth; but what guaranty have we that it shall be maintained here? What proof that some unlineal hand, some barbarism, without or within, shall not wrench the sceptre of democracy from our grasp? The rule of princes, the privilege of birth, has come down through the ages; the rule of the people has not yet marked a century and a half. There is no absolute proof, no positive guaranty, but there is hope and high expectation, and the path is not uncharted.

It may be some help to know that, however much of glory, there is no magic in American democracy. Let us examine some more of this Declaration of ours, and examine it in the light of the events of those solemn days in which it was adopted.

---

* Alaric I, the first king of the Visigoths, led the sack of Rome in 410.

Men of every clime have lavished much admiration upon the first part of the Declaration of Independence, and rightly so, for it marked the entry of new forces and new ideals into human affairs. Its admirers have sometimes failed in their attempts to live by it, but none have successfully disputed its truth. It is the realization of the true glory and worth of man, which, when once admitted, wrought vast changes that have marked all history since its day. All this relates to natural rights, fascinating to dwell upon, but not sufficient to live by. The signers knew that well; more important still, the people whom they represented knew it. So they did not stop there. After asserting that man was to stand out in the universe with a new and supreme importance, and that governments were instituted to insure life, liberty, and the pursuit of happiness, they did not shrink from the logical conclusion of this doctrine. They knew that the duty between the citizen and the State was reciprocal. They knew that the State called on its citizens for their property and their lives; they laid down the proposition that government was to protect the citizen in his life, liberty, and pursuit of happiness. At some expense? Yes. Those prudent and thrifty men had no false notions about incurring expense. They knew the value of increasing their material resources, but they knew that prosperity was a means, not an end. At cost of life? Yes. These sons of the Puritans, of the Huguenots, of the men of Londonderry, braved exile to secure peace, but they were not afraid to die in defence of their convictions.* They put no limit on what the State must do for the citizen in his hour of need. While they required all, they gave all. Let us read their conclusion in their own words, and mark its simplicity and majesty: "And for the support of this Declaration, with a firm reliance on the protection of Divine Providence, we mutually pledge to each other our lives, our fortunes, and our sacred honor." There is no cringing reservation here, no alternative, and no delay. Here is the voice of the plain men of Middlesex, promising Yorktown, promising Appomattox.

The doctrine of the Declaration of Independence, predicated upon the glory of man, and the corresponding duty of society, is that the rights of citizens are to be protected with every power and resource of the State, and a government that does any less is false to the teachings of that great document, of the name American. Beyond this, the principle that it is the obligation of the people to rise and overthrow government which fails in these respects. But above all, the call to duty, the pledge of fortune and of life, nobility of character through nobility of action: this is Americanism.

---

* In the early seventeenth century, the Puritans fled religious persecution in England, leaving first for Holland and later for the New World. The Protestant Huguenots endured persecution for three centuries in Catholic France; many escaped to other parts of Europe, to Africa, and to America. In 1689, after being deposed as British king, the Catholic James II laid siege to the Protestant stronghold of Londonderry in what is now Northern Ireland. The defiant city withstood the siege for 105 days.

"Woe for us if we forget, we that hold by these."*

Herein are the teachings of this day — touching the heights of man's glory and the depths of man's duty. Here lies the path to national preservation, and there is no other. Education, the progress of science, commercial prosperity, yes, and peace, all these and their accompanying blessings are worthy and commendable objects of attainment. But these are not the end, whether these come or no; the end lies in action — action in accord with the eternal principles of the Declaration of Independence; the words of the Continental Congress, but the deeds of the Army of the Revolution.

This is the meaning of America. And it is all our own. Doctrinaires and visionaries may shudder at it. The privilege of birth may jeer at it. The practical politician may scoff at it. But the people of the Nation respond to it, and march away to Mexico to the rescue of a colored trooper† as they marched of old to the rescue of an emperor. The assertion of human rights is naught but a call to human sacrifice. This is yet the spirit of the American people. Only so long as this flame burns shall we endure and the light of liberty be shed over

---

* From Rudyard Kipling's poem "The Flowers" (1896).

† The previous month, during the U.S. Army's expedition against Mexican revolutionary Pancho Villa, Mexican forces captured twenty-three members of the Tenth Cavalry, an all-black unit. When the United States mobilized National Guard troops, the Mexican government returned the captured soldiers.

the nations of the earth. May the increase of the years increase for America only the devotion to this spirit, only the intensity of this flame, and the eternal truth of Lowell's lines:

"What were our lives without thee?
What all our lives to save thee?
We reck not what we gave thee;
We will not dare to doubt thee,
But ask whatever else and we will dare."*

---

* From James Russell Lowell's "Ode Recited at the Harvard Commemoration" (July 21, 1865).

V

RIVERSIDE

AUGUST 28, 1916

"Good government cannot be found
on the bargain-counter."

*After dominating Massachusetts politics for decades,
Republicans lost the state's annual gubernatorial election
five straight years, from 1910 through 1914. In 1915, with
Samuel W. McCall running for governor and Coolidge for
lieutenant governor, the Republicans ended the Democrats'
streak. Campaigning for reelection in 1916, Coolidge made
the case for Grand Old Party leadership in Massachusetts.*

It may be that there would be votes for the Republican Party in the promise of low taxes and vanishing
expenditures. I can see an opportunity for its candidates
to pose as the apostles of retrenchment and reform. I
am not one of those who believe votes are to be won

by misrepresentations, skilful presentations of half truths, and plausible deductions from false premises. Good government cannot be found on the bargain-counter. We have seen samples of bargain-counter government in the past when low tax rates were secured by increasing the bonded debt for current expenses or refusing to keep our institutions up to the standard in repairs, extensions, equipment, and accommodations. I refuse, and the Republican Party refuses, to endorse that method of sham and shoddy economy. New projects can wait, but the commitments of the Commonwealth must be maintained. We cannot curtail the usual appropriations or the care of mothers with dependent children or the support of the poor, the insane, and the infirm. The Democratic programme of cutting the State tax, by vetoing appropriations of the utmost urgency for improvements and maintenance costs of institutions and asylums of the unfortunates of the State, cannot be the example for a Republican administration. The result has been that our institutions are deficient in resources — even in sleeping accommodations — and it will take years to restore them to the old-time Republican efficiency. Our party will have no part in a scheme of economy which adds to the misery of the wards of the Commonwealth — the sick, the insane, and the unfortunate; those who are too weak even to protest.

Because I know these conditions I know a Republican administration would face an increasing State tax rather than not see them remedied.

The Republican Party lit the fire of progress in Massachusetts. It has tended it faithfully. It will not flicker now. It has provided here conditions of employment, and safeguards for health, that are surpassed nowhere on earth. There will be no backward step. The reuniting of the Republican Party* means no reaction in the protection of women and children in our industrial life. These laws are settled. These principles are established. Minor modifications are possible, but the foundations are not to be disturbed. The advance may have been too rapid in some cases, but there can be no retreat. That is the position of the great majority of those who constitute our party.

We recognize there is need of relief — need to our industries, need to our population in manufacturing centres; but it must come from construction, not from destruction. Put an administration on Beacon Hill† that can conserve our resources, that can protect us from further injuries, until a national Republican policy can restore those conditions of confidence and prosperity under which our advance began and under which it can be resumed.‡

---

* In 1912, former president Theodore Roosevelt formed the Progressive Party after he lost the Republican presidential nomination to William Howard Taft. The Bull Moose Party, as it was nicknamed, ran candidates for Massachusetts governor from 1912 through 1914, but the party fell apart after that.

† The Massachusetts State House sits on Boston's Beacon Hill.

‡ Republicans held the White House from 1897 until 1913. Democrat Woodrow Wilson broke the streak in the 1912 election, when he defeated incumbent William Howard Taft and Bull Moose candidate Theodore Roosevelt.

This makes the coming State election take on a most important aspect — not that it can furnish all the needed relief, but that it will increase the probability of a complete relief in the near future if it be crowned with Republican victory.

VI

AT THE HOME OF
AUGUSTUS P. GARDNER,
HAMILTON

SEPTEMBER, 1916

"We are citizens before we are partisans."

*Congressman Augustus Peabody Gardner helped guide
Coolidge's successful 1915 campaign for lieutenant governor.
Gardner also became a leader of the Preparedness movement, which called for building up the U.S. military in the
event the United States needed to join the Great War. Here,
at Gardner's home in Hamilton, Massachusetts, Coolidge
discusses "preparedness" in a different context.*

Standing here in the presence of our host, our
thoughts naturally turn to a discussion of "Preparedness." I do not propose to overlook that issue; but I shall
offer suggestions of another kind of "preparedness." Not
that I shrink from full and free consideration of the

41

military needs of our country. Nor do I agree that it is now necessary to remain silent regarding the domestic or foreign relations of this Nation.

I agree that partisanship should stop at the boundary line, but I assert that patriotism should begin there. Others, however, have covered this field, and I leave it to them and to you.

I do, however, propose to discuss the "preparedness" of the State to care for its unfortunates. And I propose to do this without any party bias and without blame upon any particular individual, but in just criticism of a system.

In Massachusetts, we are citizens before we are partisans. The good name of the Commonwealth is of more moment to us than party success. But unfortunately, because of existing conditions, that good name, in one particular at least, is now in jeopardy.

Massachusetts, for twenty years, has been able honestly to boast of the care it has bestowed upon her sick, poor, and insane. Her institutions have been regarded as models throughout the world. We are falling from that proud estate; crowded housing conditions, corridors used for sleeping purposes, are not only not unusual, but are coming to be the accepted standard. The heads of asylums complain that maintenance and the allowance for food supply and supervision are being skimped.

On August 1 of this year, the institutions throughout the State housed more than 700 patients above what they were designed to accommodate, and I am told the crowding is steadily increasing. That is one reason I have been at pains to set forth that I do not see the way clear to make a radical reduction in the annual State budget.* I now repeat that declaration, in spite of contradiction, because I know the citizens of this State have no desire for economies gained at such a sacrifice. The people have no stomach for retrenchment of that sort.

A charge of overcrowding, which must mean a lack of care, is not to be carelessly made. You are entitled to facts, as well as phrases. I gave the whole number now confined in our institutions above the stated capacity as over 700. About August 1, Danvers had 1530 in an institution of 1350 capacity. Northampton, my home town, had 913, in a hospital built for 819. In Boston State Hospital, there were 1572, where the capacity was 1406. Westboro had 1260 inmates, with capacity for 1161, and Medfield had 1615, where the capacity was 1542. These capacities are given from official recorded accommodations.

This was not the practice of the past, and there can be no question as to where the responsibility rests. The General Court has done its best,† but there has been a halt elsewhere. A substantial appropriation was made for a new State Hospital for the Metropolitan District, and

---

* Such statements did not come easily to Coolidge, who emphasized government thrift. ("I am for economy," he would say as president. "After that I am for more economy.") But with Massachusetts Democrats blocking spending for homes for the mentally ill, he defended the Republicans' plans.

† The General Court is the Massachusetts state legislature.

an additional appropriation for a new institution for the feeble-minded in the western part of the State. In its desire to hasten matters, the legislature went even further and granted money for plans for a new hospital in the Metropolitan District, to relieve part of the outside congestion, but the needed relief is still in the future.

I feel the time has come when the people must assert themselves and show that they will tolerate no delay and no parsimony in the care of our unfortunates. Restore the fame of our State in the handling of these problems to its former lustre.

I repeat that this is not partisan. I am not criticising individuals. I am denouncing a system. When you substitute patronage for patriotism, administration breaks down. We need more of the Office Desk and less of the Show Window in politics. Let men in office substitute the midnight oil for the limelight. Let Massachusetts return to the sound business methods which were exemplified in the past by such Democrats in the East as Governor Gaston and Governor Douglas, and by such Republicans in the West as Governor Robinson and Governor Crane.*

---

* In 1874, William Gaston became the first Massachusetts Democrat elected governor after the Civil War. William Lewis Douglas secured the governorship in the 1904 election, the only Democrat to do so between 1893 and 1909. Republican George D. Robinson won three straight terms as governor, from 1883 through 1885. Winthrop Murray Crane, born into the family of the famous paper company, likewise won three terms as governor, elected in

Above all, let us not, in our haste to prepare for war, forget to prepare for peace. The issue is with you. You can, by your votes, show what system you stamp with the approval of enlightened Massachusetts Public Opinion.

1899, 1900, and 1901. He later served as U.S. senator and became a mentor to Coolidge.

VII

LAFAYETTE BANQUET, FALL RIVER

September 4, 1916

"[The American Revolution] was not the old lust of conquest, not the sullen roar of hatred and revenge, but a higher, clearer note of a people asserting their inalienable sovereignty."

Coolidge admired the Marquis de Lafayette, the aristocrat who traveled from France to help lead the American Revolution. In 1924, as president, Coolidge would dedicate Baltimore's Lafayette Monument. Here he recalls Massachusetts's vital role in the Revolution, which helped draw Lafayette to the cause.

Seemingly trifling events oft carry in their train great consequences. The firing of a gun in the backwoods of Pennsylvania, Macaulay tells us, started the Seven Years' War which set the world in conflagration,*

---

* British historian Thomas Babington Macaulay wrote, "The firing of a gun in the backwoods of America brought a war that drenched Europe with blood." The line refers to the May 1754 raid in western Pennsylvania in which

causing men to fight each other on every shore of the
seven seas and giving new masters to the most ancient
of empires. We see to-day fifteen nations engaged in the
most terrific war in the history of the human race and
trace its origin to the bullet of a madman fired in the
Balkans.* It is true that the flintlock gun at Lexington
was not the first, nor yet the last, to fire a "shot heard
round the world." It was not the distance it travelled, but
the message it carried which has marked it out above
all other human events. It was the character of that
message which claimed the attention of him we this
day honor, in the far-off fortress of the now famous
Metz†; it was because it roused in the listener a sympa-
thetic response that it was destined to link forever the
events of Concord and Lexington and Bunker Hill and
Dorchester Heights, in our Commonwealth, with the
name of Lafayette.

For there was a new tone in those Massachusetts
guns. It was not the old lust of conquest, not the sullen
roar of hatred and revenge, but a higher, clearer note

Virginia militiamen and Native American warriors ambushed French soldiers.
The skirmish, led by a twenty-two-year-old lieutenant colonel named George
Washington, marked the opening of the French and Indian War. That conflict
expanded into the Seven Years' War, which pitted Britain against France and
saw fighting on five continents.

* The United States would not enter the Great War until April 1917. The
"bullet of a madman fired in the Balkans" refers to Gavrilo Princip's assassination of Archduke Franz Ferdinand of Austria on June 28, 1914.

† The Marquis de Lafayette decided to join the American cause in 1775 at
a regimental reception in Metz.

of a people asserting their inalienable sovereignty. It is a happy circumstance that one of our native-born, Benjamin Franklin,* was instrumental in bringing Lafayette to America; but beyond that it is fitting at this time to give a thought to our Commonwealth because his ideals, his character, his life, were all in sympathy with that great Revolution which was begun within her borders and carried to a successful conclusion by the sacrifice of her treasure and her blood. It was not the able legal argument of James Otis against the British Writs of Assistance, nor the petitions and remonstrances of the Colonists to the British throne, admirable though they were, that aroused the approbation and brought his support to our cause. It was not alone that he agreed with the convictions of the Continental Congress. He saw in the example of Massachusetts a people who would shrink from no sacrifice to defend rights which were beyond price. It was not the Tories, fleeing to Canada, that attracted him. It was the patriots, bearing arms, and he brought them not a pen but a sword.

"Resistance to tyranny is obedience to law,"† and

---

* Franklin was born in Boston; he moved to Philadelphia at age seventeen.

† During the Revolutionary War, American newspapers printed a line that supposedly served as the epitaph of John Bradshaw, who had presided over the trial that sentenced England's King Charles I to death. The line read, "Rebellion to tyrants is obedience to God." That attribution may have been apocryphal, but both Benjamin Franklin and Thomas Jefferson so admired the maxim that they proposed to include it in the seal of the United States. Their proposal did not carry, but Jefferson later made the quotation part of his personal seal. A

"obedience to law is liberty."* Those are the foundations of the Commonwealth. It was these principles in action which appealed to that young captain of dragoons and brought the sword and resources of the aristocrat to battle for democracy. I love to think of his connection with our history. I love to think of him at the dedication of the Bunker Hill Monument receiving the approbation of the Nation from the lips of Daniel Webster.† I love to think of the long line of American citizens of French blood in our Commonwealth to-day, ready to defend the principles he fought for, "Liberty under the Law," citizens who, like him, look not with apology, but with respect and approval and admiration on that sentiment inscribed on the white flag of Massachusetts, *"Ense petit placidam sub libertate quietem"* (With a sword she seeks secure peace under liberty).

---

variation, "Resistance to tyranny is obedience to God" (still different from what Coolidge says here), is often attributed to John Knox, the sixteenth-century Scottish theologian.

    * This line is often attributed to Boethius, the statesman and philosopher of early sixth-century Rome.

    † Lafayette laid the cornerstone for the monument on June 17, 1825, the fiftieth anniversary of the Battle of Bunker Hill. Senator Daniel Webster of Massachusetts gave a stirring address that showed why some admirers called him the "blazing star of the East."

VIII

NORFOLK REPUBLICAN CLUB, BOSTON

OCTOBER 9, 1916

"[The Republican Party will] ever stand
opposed to the establishment of one class
who shall live on the Government, and
another class who shall pay the taxes."

*In state government, Coolidge was less of a budgeteer than
he would be as president. This difference did not necessarily reflect a change in attitude over time. Rather, Coolidge
believed, as did many others in his day, that state and local
governments were better suited to social endeavors than was
Washington, so far away from many of its citizens. At the
time, the social safety net that we know today did not exist.
Here Lieutenant Governor Coolidge, on the campaign trail,
outlines his philosophy on providing "social insurance" —
including the limits of what any government, state or local,
can achieve.*

L ast night at Somerville I spoke on some of the
fundamental differences between the Republican
and Democratic policies, and showed how we were
dependent on Republican principles as a foundation on
which to erect any advance in our social and economic
welfare.

This year the Republican Party has adopted a very
advanced platform. That was natural, for we have always
been the party of progress, and have given our attention
to that, when we were not engaged in a life-and-death
struggle to overcome the fallacies put forth by our opponents, with which we are all so familiar. The result has
been that here in Massachusetts, where our party has
ever been strong, and where we have framed legislation
for more than fifty years, more progress has been made
along the lines of humanitarian legislation than in any
other State. We have felt free to call on our industries
to make large outlays along these lines because we have
furnished them with the advantages of a protective tar-
iff* and an honest and efficient state government. The
consequences have been that in this State the hours and
conditions of labor have been better than anywhere else
on earth. Those provisions for safety, sanitation, compen-
sations for accidents, and for good living conditions have
now been almost entirely worked out. There remains,

---

* Although Coolidge displayed an intuitive sympathy for free markets,
he supported tariffs to protect American businesses. His pro-tariff philosophy
matched that of the Republican Party of his era.

however, the condition of sickness, age, misfortune, lack of employment, or some other cause, that temporarily renders people unable to care for themselves. Our platform has taken up this condition.

We have long been familiar with insurance to cover losses. You will readily recall the different kinds. Formerly it was only used in commerce, by the well-to-do. Recently it has been adapted to the use of all our people by the great industrial companies which have been very successful. Our State has adopted a system of savings-bank insurance, thus reducing the expense.* Now, social insurance will not be, under a Republican interpretation, any new form of outdoor relief, some new scheme of living on the town. It will be an extension of the old familiar principle to the needs at hand, and so popularized as to meet the requirements of our times.†

It ought to be understood, however, that there can be no remedy for lack of industry and thrift, secured by law. It ought to be understood that no scheme of insurance and no scheme of government aid is likely to make us all prosperous. And above all, these remedies must go forward on the firm foundation of an independent,

---

* In 1907, Massachusetts passed a law permitting savings banks to issue life insurance. The goal was to reduce the costs of such insurance for working people. In a 1920 letter, Governor Coolidge said the law ensured "that life insurance for the person of small means should be conducted as a social service and not as a commercial undertaking."

† In 1916, federal assistance programs such as Social Security, Medicare, Medicaid, and welfare remained decades away.

self-supporting, self-governing people. But we do honestly put forward a proposition for the relief of misfortune.

The Republican Party is proposing humanitarian legislation to build up character, to establish independence, not pauperism; it will in the future, as in the past, ever stand opposed to the establishment of one class who shall live on the Government, and another class who shall pay the taxes. To those who fear we are turning Socialists, and to those who think we are withholding just and desirable public aid and support, I say that government under the Republican Party will continue in the future to be so administered as to breed not mendicants, but men. Humanitarian legislation is going to be the handmaid of character.

IX

PUBLIC MEETING ON THE HIGH COST OF LIVING, FANEUIL HALL

DECEMBER 9, 1916

"The great aim of American institutions
is the protection of the individual."

*Although the United States would not enter the Great War
until 1917, wartime inflation was already stinging Americans when Coolidge delivered this speech. According to
the Bureau of Labor Statistics, prices for basic foodstuffs
rose by 12 percent nationwide in 1916. In Boston, the price of
sugar increased more than 40 percent. The same government
report quoted a Boston baker saying: "Flour and shortening
double usual prices. Everything high. Probably selling at a
loss. Conditions worse than ever." In this speech at Boston's
Faneuil Hall, Coolidge makes the case that the government
must punish illegal activity by speculators. Some evidence
exists that Coolidge's view on government intervention into
pricing evolved after the war. A few years after this speech,*

Coolidge would comment to advertising executive Bruce
Barton, "Isn't it a strange thing that in every period of social
unrest men have a notion that they can pass a law and sus-
pend the operations of economic law?"

The great aim of American institutions is the protection of the individual. That is the principle which
lies at the foundation of Anglo-Saxon liberty. It matters not with what power the individual is assailed, nor
whether that power is represented by wealth or place or
numbers; against it the humblest American citizen has
the right to the protection of his Government by every
force that Government can command.

This right would be but half expressed if it ran only
to a remedy after a wrong is inflicted; it should and does
run to the prevention of a wrong which is threatened.
We find our citizens, to-day, not so much suffering from
the high cost of living, though that is grievous enough,
as threatened with an increasing cost which will bring
suffering and misery to a large body of our inhabitants.
So we come here not only to discuss providing a remedy
for what is now existing, but some protection to ward
off what is threatening to be a worse calamity. We shall
utterly fail of our purpose to provide relief unless we
look at things as they are. It is useless to indulge in
indiscriminate abuse. We must not confuse the innocent
with the guilty; it must be our object to allay suspicion,
not to create it. The great body of our tradespeople are

honest and conscientious, anxious to serve their customers for a fair return for their service. We want their coöperation in our pursuit of facts; we want to coöperate with them in proposing and securing a remedy. We do not deny the existence of economic laws, nor the right to profit by a change of conditions.

But we do claim the right and duty of the Government to investigate and punish any artificial creation of high prices by means of illegal monopolies or restraints of trade. And above all, we claim the right of publicity. That is a remedy with an arm longer and stronger than that of the law. Let us know what is going on and the remedy will provide itself. In working along this line we shall have great help from the newspapers. The American people are prepared to meet any reasonable burden; they are not asking for charity or favor; fair prices and fair profits they will gladly pay; but they demand information that they are fair, and an immediate reduction if they are not.

The Commonwealth has just provided money for an investigation by a competent commission. Its Police Department, its Law Department, are also at the service of our citizens. Let us refrain from suspicion; let us refrain from all indiscriminate blame; but let us present at once to the proper authorities all facts and all evidence of unfair practices. Let all our merchants, of whatever degree, assist in this work for the public good and let the individual see and feel that all his rights are protected by his Government.

X

ONE HUNDREDTH ANNIVERSARY DINNER OF THE PROVIDENT INSTITUTION FOR SAVINGS

DECEMBER 13, 1916

"They were the men who had fought a
war to limit the power of government and
enlarge the privileges of the individual."

*In 1816, Boston's Provident Institution for Savings became
the first savings bank to incorporate in the United States.
Speaking at the bank's centennial dinner, Coolidge praises
the spirit of "self-reliance" and "independence" that ani-
mates Provident and other free-market ventures.*

T he history of the institution we here celebrate
reaches back more than one third of the way to
the landing of the *Mayflower* — back to the day of
the men who signed the Declaration of Independence,
who saw Prescott, Pomeroy, Stark, and Warren at Bunker
Hill, who followed Washington and his generals from
Dorchester Heights to Yorktown, and saw the old Bay

Colony become the Commonwealth of Massachusetts.*
They had seen a nation in the making. They founded
their government on the rights of the individual. They
had no hesitation in defending those rights against the
invasion of a British King and Parliament, by a Revolutionary War, nor in criticising their own Government
at Washington when they thought an invasion of those
rights was again threatened by the preliminaries and
the prosecution of the War of 1812.† They had made
the Commonwealth. They understood its Government.
They knew it was a part of themselves, their own organization. They had not acquired the state of mind that
enabled them to stand aloof and regard government as
something apart and separate from the people. It would
never have occurred to them that they could not trans-

---

* Coolidge underscores the central role Massachusetts and its people
played in America's Founding. His discussion of the Battle of Bunker Hill
(June 17, 1775) references the American commander, Colonel William Prescott;
Seth Pomeroy, who — at age sixty-nine — served as a senior officer in the
Massachusetts militia but volunteered to fight with the infantry at Bunker
Hill; John Stark, who led his New Hampshire militia to reinforce Prescott and
repelled the British along the left flank; and Joseph Warren, a Massachusetts
revolutionary leader who, like Pomeroy, refused a command and volunteered
with the infantry. Warren was killed in combat, a moment that John Trumbull
later immortalized in a painting.

† The War of 1812 faced fierce opposition in Massachusetts. Dissatisfaction
with the war proved to be a driving force behind the Hartford Convention of
late 1814 and early 1815. At that secret convention, New England Federalists
considered seceding from the Union but ultimately issued a list of grievances
against the federal government.

act for themselves any other business just as well as they could transact for themselves the business of government. They were the men who had fought a war to limit the power of government and enlarge the privileges of the individual.

It was the same spirit that made Massachusetts that made the Provident Institution for Savings.* What the men of that day wanted they made for themselves. They would never have thought of asking Congress to keep their money in the post-office. They did not want their commercial privileges interfered with by having the Government buy and sell for them. They had the self-reliance and the independence to prefer to do those things for themselves. This is the spirit that founded Massachusetts, the spirit that has seen your bank grow until it could now probably purchase all there was of property in the Commonwealth when it began its existence. I want to see that spirit still preëminent here. I want to see a deeper realization on the part of the people that this is their Commonwealth, their Government; that they control it, that they pay its expenses, that it is, after all, only a part of themselves; that any attempt to shift upon it their duties, their responsibilities, or their support will in the end only delude,

---

* Tracing Coolidge's activity in this period, one espies the importance of his key backer, the merchant Frank W. Stearns. Stearns held an interest in the Provident.

degrade, impoverish, and enslave. Your institution points the only way, through self-control, self-denial, and self-support, to self-government, to independence, to a more generous liberty, and to a firmer establishment of individual rights.

XI

ASSOCIATED INDUSTRIES DINNER, BOSTON

DECEMBER 15, 1916

"There is just one condition on which men can
secure employment and a living, nourishing,
profitable wage,... and that condition is
that some one make a profit by it."

*By the second decade of the twentieth century, progressivism
and socialism had made their marks on American politics. In
the 1912 presidential election, the trust-busting Progressive
Party candidate, Theodore Roosevelt, had finished second,
while Socialist Party candidate Eugene V. Debs won 6 percent of the vote. In this address to a trade group representing
small businesses, Lieutenant Governor Coolidge challenges
Progressives and extols the virtues of free enterprise.*

During the past few years we have questioned the
soundness of many principles that had for a long
time been taken for granted. We have examined the
foundations of our institutions of government. We have

debated again the theories of the men who wrote the Declaration of Independence, the Constitution of the Nation, and laid down the fundamental law of our own Commonwealth. Along with this examination of our form of government has gone an examination of our social, industrial, and economic system. What is to come out of it all?

In the last fifty years we have had a material prosperity in this country the like of which was never beheld before. A prosperity which not only built up great industries, great transportation systems, great banks and a great commerce, but a prosperity under whose influence arts and sciences, education and charity flourished most abundantly. It was little wonder that men came to think that prosperity was the chief end of man and grew arrogant in the use of its power. It was little wonder that such a misunderstanding arose that one part of the community thought the owners and managers of our great industries were robbers, or that they thought some of the people meant to confiscate all property. It has been a costly investigation, but if we can arrive at a better understanding of our economic and social laws it will be worth all it cost.

As a part of this discussion we have had many attempts at regulation of industrial activity by law. Some of it has proceeded on the theory that if those who enjoyed material prosperity used it for wrong purposes, such prosperity should be limited or abolished. That is as sound as it would be to abolish writing to prevent forgery. We need to keep forever in mind that guilt is personal; if there is to be punishment let it fall on the evil-doer, let us not condemn the instrument. We need power. Is the steam engine too strong? Is electricity too swift? Can any prosperity be too great? Can any instrument of commerce or industry ever be too powerful to serve the public needs? What then of the anti-trust laws?* They are sound in theory. Their assemblances of wealth are broken up because they were assembled for an unlawful purpose. It is the purpose that is condemned. You men who represent our industries can see that there is the same right to disperse unlawful assembling of wealth or power that there is to disperse a mob that has met to lynch or riot. But that principle does not denounce town-meetings or prayer-meetings.

We have established here a democracy on the principle that all men are created equal. It is our endeavor to extend equal blessings to all. It can be done approximately if we establish the correct standards. We are coming to see that we are dependent upon commercial and industrial prosperity, not only for the creation of wealth, but for the solving of the great problem of the

---

* In 1914, Congress passed and President Woodrow Wilson signed two anti-trust laws, the Federal Trade Commission Act and the Clayton Antitrust Act. These two acts, together with the Sherman Antitrust Act of 1890, still form the core of federal antitrust law. The Federal Trade Commission succeeded an agency President Theodore Roosevelt had created, the Bureau of Corporations.

distribution of wealth. There is just one condition on which men can secure employment and a living, nourishing, profitable wage, for whatever they contribute to the enterprise, be it labor or capital, and that condition is that some one make a profit by it. That is the sound basis for the distribution of wealth and the only one. It cannot be done by law, it cannot be done by public ownership, it cannot be done by socialism. When you deny the right to a profit you deny the right of a reward to thrift and industry.

The scientists tell us that the same force that rounds the teardrop moulds the earth. Physical laws have their analogy in social and industrial life. The law that builds up the people is the law that builds up industry. What price could the millions, who have found the inestimable blessings of American citizenship around our great industrial centres, after coming here from lands of oppression, afford to pay to those who organized those industries? Shall we not recognize the great service they have done the cause of humanity? Have we not seen what happens to industry, to transportation, to all commercial activity which we call business when profit fails? Have we not seen the suffering and misery which it entails upon the people?

Let us recognize the source of these fundamental principles and not hesitate to assert them. Let us frown upon greed and selfishness, but let us also condemn envy and uncharitableness. Let us have done with misunderstandings, let us strive to realize the dream of democracy by a prosperity of industry that shall mean the prosperity of the people, by a strengthening of our material resources that shall mean a strengthening of our character, by a merchandising that has for its end manhood, and womanhood, the ideal of American Citizenship.

XII

ON THE NATURE OF POLITICS

"Politics is the process of action in public affairs."

The original edition of Have Faith in Massachusetts *did not provide a dateline for this speech. Perhaps the editors did not want to call attention to the fact that they presented it out of chronological order. Coolidge delivered the address on May 12, 1915, at a dinner of Amherst College alumni at Boston's Algonquin Club. This speech, outlining his views on public service, "launched the boom of Coolidge for Lieutenant Governor," an early biographer reported.*

P olitics is not an end, but a means. It is not a product, but a process. It is the art of government. Like other values it has its counterfeits. So much emphasis has been put upon the false that the significance of the true has been obscured and politics has come to convey the meaning of crafty and cunning selfishness, instead of candid and sincere service. The Greek derivation shows the nobler purpose. *Politikos* means city-rearing, state-craft. And when we remember that city also meant civilization, the spurious presentment, mean and sordid, drops away and the real figure of the politician, dignified and honorable, a minister to civilization, author and finisher of government, is revealed in its true and dignified proportions.

There is always something about genius that is indefinable, mysterious, perhaps to its possessor most of all. It has been the product of rude surroundings no less than of the most cultured environment, want and neglect have sometimes nourished it, abundance and care have failed to produce it. Why some succeed in public life and others fail would be as difficult to tell as why some succeed or fail in other activities. Very few men in America have started out with any fixed idea of entering public life, fewer still would admit having such an idea. It was said of Chief Justice Waite, of the United States Supreme Court, being asked when a youth what he proposed to do when a man, he replied, he had not yet decided whether to be President or Chief Justice.* This may be in part

---

* Morrison Waite served as chief justice of the United States from 1874 to 1888. The son of a judge, Waite went to Yale and joined the exclusive Skull and Bones society. He became a prominent lawyer in Ohio and twice ran, unsuccessfully, for the U.S. Senate.

due to a general profession of holding to the principle of Benjamin Franklin that office should neither be sought nor refused and in part to the American idea that the people choose their own officers so that public service is not optional. In other countries this is not so. For centuries some seats in the British Parliament were controlled and probably sold as were commissions in the army, but that has never been the case here. A certain Congressman, however, on arriving at Washington was asked by an old friend how he happened to be elected. He replied that he was not elected, but appointed. It is worth while noting that the boss who was then supposed to hold the power of appointment in that district has since been driven from power, but the Congressman, though he was defeated when his party was lately divided, has been reëlected. All of which suggests that the boss did not appoint in the first instance, but was merely well enough informed to see what the people wanted before they had formulated their own opinions and desires. It was said of McKinley* that he could tell what Congress would do on a certain measure before the men in Congress themselves knew what their decision was to be. Cannon† has said of McKinley that his ear was so close to the

---

* William McKinley served as president of the United States from 1897 until his assassination in 1901.

† Joseph Gurney Cannon represented Illinois in the U.S. House of Representatives for almost five decades. He served as Speaker of the House from 1903 to 1911.

ground that it was full of grasshoppers. But the fact remains that office brokerage is here held in reprehensive scorn and professional office-seeking in contempt. Every native-born American, however, is potentially a President, and it must always be remembered that the obligation to serve the State is forever binding upon all, although office is the gift of the people.

Of course these considerations relate not to appointive places like the Judiciary, Commissionerships, clerical positions and like places, but to the more important elective offices. Another reason why political life of this nature is not chosen as a career is that it does not pay. Nearly all offices of this class are held at a financial sacrifice, not merely that the holder could earn more at some other occupation, but that the salary of the office does not maintain the holder of the office. It is but recently that Parliament has paid a salary to its members. In years gone by the United States Senate has been rather marked for its number of rich men. Few prominent members of Congress are dependent on their salary, which is but another way of saying that in Washington Senators and Representatives need more than their official salaries to become most effective. It is a consolation to be able to state that this is not the condition of members of the Massachusetts General Court. There, ability and character come very near to being the sole requirements for success. Although some men have seen service in our legislature of nearly twenty years, to the great benefit of the Commonwealth, no one would choose that for a career and these men doubtless look on it only as an avocation.*

For these reasons we have no profession of politics or of public life in the sense that we have a profession of law and medicine and other learned callings. We have men who have spent many years in office, but it would be difficult to find one outside the limitations noted who would refer to that as his business, occupation, or profession.

The inexperienced are prone to hold an erroneous idea of public life and its methods. Not long ago I listened to a joint debate in a prominent preparatory school. Each side took it for granted that public men were influenced only by improper motives and that officials of the government were seeking only their own gain and advantage without regard to the welfare of the people. Such a presumption has no foundation in fact. There are dishonest men in public office. There are quacks, shysters, and charlatans among doctors, lawyers, and clergy, but they are not representative of their professions nor indicative of their methods. Our public men, as a class, are inspired by honorable and patriotic motives, desirous only of a faithful execution of their trust from the executive and legislative branches of the States and Nation down to the executives of our towns,

* See also Governor Coolidge's "Veto of Salary Increase," page 167.

who bear the dignified and significant title of selectmen. Public men must expect criticism and be prepared to endure false charges from their opponents. It is a matter of no great concern to them. But public confidence in government is a matter of great concern. It cannot be maintained in the face of such opinions as I have mentioned. It is necessary to differentiate between partisan assertions and actual conditions. It is necessary to recognize worth as well as to condemn graft. No system of government can stand that lacks public confidence and no progress can be made on the assumption of a false premise. Public administration is honest and sound and public business is transacted on a higher plane than private business.

There is no difficulty for men in college to understand elections and government. They have all had experience in it. The same motives that operate in the choice of class officers operate in choosing officers for the Commonwealth. Here men are soon estimated at their true worth. Here places of trust are conferred and administered as they will be in later years. The scale is smaller, the opportunities are less, conditions are more artificial, but the principles are the same. Of course the present estimate is not the ultimate. There are men here who appear important that will not appear so in years to come. There are men who seem insignificant now who will develop at a later day. But the motive which leads to elections here leads to elections in the State.

Is there any especial obligation on the part of college-bred men to be candidates for public office? I do not think so. It is said that although college graduates constitute but one per cent of the population, they hold about fifty per cent of the public offices, so that this question seems to take care of itself. But I do not feel that there is any more obligation to run for office than there is to become a banker, a merchant, a teacher, or enter any other special occupation. As indicated some men have a particular aptitude in this direction and some have none. Of course experience counts here as in any other human activity, and all experience worth the name is the result of application, of time and thought and study and practice. If the individual finds he has liking and capacity for this work, he will involuntarily find himself engaged in it. There is no catalogue of such capacity. One man gets results in one way, another in another. But in general only the man of broad sympathy and deep understanding of his fellow men can meet with much success.

What I have said relates to the somewhat narrow field of office-holding. This is really a small part of the American system or of any system. James Bryce tells us that we have a government of public opinion.* That is growing to be more and more true of the governments

---

* The historian and politician James Bryce served as British ambassador to the United States from 1907 to 1913. In his classic work *The American Commonwealth* (1888), Bryce wrote, "Nowhere is the rule of public opinion so complete as in America, or so direct."

of the entire world. The first care of despotism seems to be to control the school and the press. Where the mind is free it turns not to force but to reason for the source of authority. Men submit to a government of force as we are doing now when they believe it is necessary for their security, necessary to protect them from the imposition of force from without. This is probably the main motive of the German people. They have been taught that their only protection lay in the support of a military despotism. Rightly or wrongly they have believed this and believing have submitted to what they suppose their only means of security. They have been governed accordingly. Germany is still feudal.*

This leads to the larger and all important field of politics. Here we soon see that office-holding is the incidental, but the standard of citizenship is the essential. Government does rest upon the opinions of men. Its results rest on their actions. This makes every man a politician whether he will or no. This lays the burden on us all. Men who have had the advantages of liberal culture ought to be the leaders in maintaining the standards of citizenship. Unless they can and do accomplish this result education is a failure. Greatly have they been taught, greatly must they teach. The power to think is

---

* Kaiser Wilhelm II had served as emperor of Germany and king of Prussia since 1888. During the Great War, his generals assumed a dominant role, essentially establishing a military dictatorship. The kaiser would be forced to abdicate in late 1918.

the most practical thing in the world. It is not and cannot be cloistered from politics.

We live under a republican form of government. We need forever to remember that representative government does represent. A careless, indifferent representative is the result of a careless, indifferent electorate. The people who start to elect a man to get what he can for his district will probably find they have elected a man who will get what he can for himself. A body will keep on its course for a time after the moving impulse ceases by reason of its momentum. The men who founded our government had fought and thought mightily on the relationship of man to his government. Our institutions would go for a time under the momentum they gave. But we should be deluded if we supposed they can be maintained without more of the same stern sacrifice offered in perpetuity. Government is not an edifice that the founders turn over to posterity all completed. It is an institution, like a university which fails unless the process of education continues.

The State is not founded on selfishness. It cannot maintain itself by the offer of material rewards. It is the opportunity for service. There has of late been held out the hope that government could by legislation remove from the individual the need of effort. The managers of industries have seemed to think that their difficulties could be removed and prosperity ensured by changing the laws. The employee has been led to believe that his condition could be made easy by the same method. When industries can be carried on without any struggle, their results will be worthless, and when wages can be secured without any effort they will have no purchasing value. In the end the value of the product will be measured by the amount of effort necessary to secure it. Our late Dr. Garman* recognized this limitation in one of his lectures where he says: ——

"Critics have noticed three stages in the development of human civilization. First: the let-alone policy; every man to look out for number one. This is the age of selfishness. Second: the opposite pole of thinking; every man to do somebody's else work for him. This is the dry rot of sentimentality that feeds tramps and enacts poor laws such as excite the indignation of Herbert Spencer.† But the third stage is represented by our formula: every man must render and receive the best possible service, except in the case of inequality, and there the strong must help the weak to help themselves; only on this condition is help given. This is the true interpretation of the life of Christ. On the first basis He would have remained in heaven and let the earth take

---

* Charles Edward Garman served as a professor at Amherst from 1882 until his death in 1907. He taught a unique blend of philosophy, politics, psychology, and ethics. Garman profoundly influenced Coolidge and many other Amherst men. "We looked upon Garman as a man who walked with God," Coolidge later wrote in his autobiography.

† The nineteenth-century British philosopher Herbert Spencer advocated social Darwinism. He coined the term "survival of the fittest."

care of itself. On the second basis He would have come to earth with his hands full of gold and silver treasures satisfying every want that unfortunate humanity could have devised. But on the third basis He comes to earth in the form of a servant who is at the same time a master commanding his disciples to take up their cross and follow Him; it is sovereignty through service as opposed to slavery through service. He refuses to make the world wealthy, but He offers to help them make themselves wealthy with true riches which shall be a hundred-fold more, even in this life, than that which was offered them by any former system."

This applies to political life no less than to industrial life. We live under the fairest government on earth. But it is not self-sustaining. Nor is that all. There are selfishness and injustice and evil in the world. More than that, these forces are never at rest. Some desire to use the processes of government for their own ends. Some desire to destroy the authority of government altogether. Our institutions are predicated on the rights and the corresponding duties, on the worth, of the individual. It is to him that we must look for safety. We may need new charters, new constitutions and new laws at times. We must always have an alert and interested citizenship. We have no dependence but the individual. New charters cannot save us. They may appear to help but the chances are that the beneficial results obtained result from an increased interest aroused by discussing changes. Laws do not make reforms, reforms make laws. We cannot look to government. We must look to ourselves. We must stand not in the expectation of a reward but with a desire to serve. There will come out of government exactly what is put into it. Society gets about what it deserves. It is the part of educated men to know and recognize these principles and influences and knowing them to inform and warn their fellow countrymen. Politics is the process of action in public affairs. It is personal, it is individual, and nothing more. Destiny is in you.

XIII

TREMONT TEMPLE

NOVEMBER 3, 1917

"While Washington was yet dumb
Massachusetts spoke."

*In 1917, the United States joined the Allied cause in the Great
War. Shortly before Election Day, Coolidge made the case
for himself and for his fellow Republicans by spelling out
Massachusetts's contributions to the war effort. Even before
Congress declared war, the state had allocated a million dollars toward defense — a huge amount that Coolidge knew
could sink the budget.*

There is a time and place for everything. There are
times when some things are out of place. Domestic
science is an important subject. So is the proper heat-
ing and ventilating of our habitations. But when the
house is on fire reasonable men do not stop to argue

of culinary cuts nor listen to a disquisition on plumbing; they call out the fire department and join it in an attempt to save their dwelling. They think only in terms of the conflagration.

So it is in this hour that has come to us so grim with destiny. We cannot stop now to discuss domestic party politics. Our men are on the firing-line of France.* There will be no party designations in the casualty lists. We cannot stop to glance at that alluring field of history that tells us of the past patriotic devotion of the men of our party to the cause of the Nation — devotion without reserve. We must think now only in terms of winning the war.

An election at this time is not of our choosing. We are having one because it is necessary under the terms of our Constitution of Massachusetts. We have not conducted the ordinary party canvass. We have not flaunted party banners, we have not burned red fire, we have not rent the air with martial music, we have not held the usual party rallies. We have addressed meetings, but such addresses have been to urge subscriptions to the Liberty Loan,† to urge gifts to the great humanitarian work of the Red Cross, and for the efforts of charity, benevolence, and mercy that are represented by the

---

* After remaining neutral in the early years of the Great War, the United States had declared war in April 1917.

† Liberty Loans were war bonds the U.S. government sold to finance the Great War.

Y.M.C.A. and by the Knights of Columbus, for the conservation of food, and for the other patriotic purposes.

But we are not to infer that this is not an important election. It is too important to think of candidates, too important to think of party, too important to think of anything but our country at war. No more important election has been held since the days of War Governor Andrew.* On Tuesday next the voters of Massachusetts will decide whether they will support the Government in its defence of America, and its defence of all that America means. There is no room for domestic party issues here. The only question for consideration is whether the Government of this Commonwealth, legislative and executive, has rendered and will render prompt and efficient support for the national defence. Perhaps it would be enough to point out that Massachusetts troops were first at the Mexican border and first in France.† But that is only part of the story.

Wars are waged now with far more than merely the troops in the field. Every resource of the people goes

---

* John Albion Andrew served as governor of Massachusetts throughout the Civil War. Under his leadership, Massachusetts became one of the first states to answer President Abraham Lincoln's call for troops. A prominent anti-slavery attorney before he entered politics, Andrew helped create one of the first all-black regiments, the 54th Massachusetts Infantry (celebrated in the 1989 film *Glory*).

† In 1916, Massachusetts had sent troops to join the Mexican Expedition, the U.S. military operation against Mexican revolutionary Pancho Villa. A year later, Massachusetts troops joined the fight in the Great War.

into the battle. It is a matter of organizing the entire fabric of society. No one has yet pointed out, no one can point out, any failure on the part of our State Government to take efficient measures for this purpose. More than that, Massachusetts did not have to be asked; while Washington was yet dumb Massachusetts spoke.

Months before war was declared a Public Safety Committee was appointed and went to work; weeks before war a conference of New England Governors was called and a million dollars was given the Governor and Council to equip Massachusetts troops for which the National Treasury had no money. By reason of this foresight our men went forth better supplied than any others, with ten dollars additional pay from their home State, and the assurance that their dependents could draw forty dollars monthly where needed for their support. The production and distribution of food and fuel have been advanced. The maintenance of industrial peace has been promoted. The Gloucester fishermen, fifteen thousand shoemakers in Lynn, the Boston & Maine railroad employees, have had their differences adjusted.* A second million dollars for emergency expenses has been given the Governor and Council. An efficient State Guard of over ten thousand men has been organized. Our brave soldiers, their dependents, the great patriotic public have been

---

* Labor agreements had recently ended these strikes, allowing continued service during a time of war.

protected by the present Government with every means that ingenuity could devise. We have won the right to reëlection by duty well performed.

Remember this: we are not responsible for the war, we are responsible for the preparation that enables us to defend our soldiers and ourselves from savages. Massachusetts is not going to repudiate these patriotic services. To do so now would mean more than repudiating the Government. It would mean repudiating the devotion of our brave men in arms, repudiating the sacrifice of the fathers, mothers, wives, and dear ones behind, and repudiating the loyalty of the millions who subscribed to the Liberty Loan, — it would mean repudiating America.

Massachusetts has decided that the path of the *Mayflower* shall not be closed. She has decided to sail the seas. She has decided to sail not under the edict of Potsdam,* crimped in narrow lanes seeking safety in unarmed merchantmen painted in fantastic hues, as the badge of an infamous servitude, but she has decided to sail under the ancient Declaration of Independence, choosing what course she will, maintaining security by the guns of ships of the line, flying at the mast the Stars and Stripes, forever the emblem of a militant liberty.

---

* In 1685, Frederick William, Elector of Brandenburg and Duke of Prussia, issued the Edict of Potsdam, offering asylum to the Huguenots, a group of French Protestants. The "Great Elector" acted in response to King Louis XIV's decision to revoke the religious protections that Catholic France had previously offered the Huguenots.

XIV

DEDICATION OF TOWN-HOUSE, WESTON

NOVEMBER 27, 1917

"Sovereignty, it is our belief, is vested
in the individual; and we are going to
protect the rights of the individual."

*Shortly after being reelected lieutenant governor, Coolidge
traveled to Weston, Massachusetts, to dedicate the new town
hall. Weston, about fifteen miles west of Boston, has a history dating to the seventeenth century, as Coolidge discusses
here. The former Northampton mayor and city councilman
also celebrates the importance of town governments.*

I was interested to come out here and take part in the
dedication of this beautiful building in part because
my ancestors had lived in this locality in times gone
past, but more especially because I am interested in the
town governments of Massachusetts. You have heard the
town-meeting referred to this evening. It seemed to me

that the towns in this Commonwealth correspond in part
to what we might call the water-tight compartments of
the ship of state, and while sometimes our State Government has wavered, sometimes it has been suspended, and
it has been thought that the people could not care for
themselves under those conditions. Whenever that has
arisen the towns of the Commonwealth have come to
the rescue and been able to furnish the foundation and
the strength on which might not only be carried on, but
on which might again be erected the failing government
of the Commonwealth or the failing government of the
Nation. So that I know nothing to which we New Englanders owe more, and especially the people of Massachusetts, of our civil liberties than we do to our form of
town government.

The history of Weston has been long and interesting,
beginning, as your town seal designates, back in 1630,
when Watertown was recognized as one of the three or
four towns in the Commonwealth; set off by boundar-
ies into the Farmers' Precinct in 1698, and becoming
incorporated as a town in 1713. There begins a long and
honorable history. Of course, the first part of it gathered
to a large degree around the church. The first church
was started here, I think, in 1695, and I believe that the
land on which it was to be erected was purchased of a
man who bore my name. Your first clergyman seems
to have been settled about 1702; and the long and even
tenor of your ways here and your devotion to things

which were established is perhaps shown and exemplified in the fact that during the next one hundred and
seventy-four years, coming clear down to 1876, you had
but six clergymen presiding over that church. You have
an example here now, along the same line, in the long
tenure of office that has come to your present town
clerk, he having been first elected, I believe, in 1864 and
having held office from that time to this, probably serv-
ing as long, if not longer, than any of the town clerks
of Massachusetts, certainly, I believe, the longest of any
present living town clerk.*

There are many interesting things connected with
the history of this town. It bore its part in the Indian
Wars. Here was organized an Indian fighting expedition
that went to the North, and, though some of the men
in that expedition were lost and the expedition was not
altogether successful, it showed the spirit, the resolution,
the bravery, and the courage which animated the men
of those days.

Mr. Young† has referred to that day in Massachusetts
history that we are all so proud of, the Nineteenth of
April, 1775.‡ But you had an interesting event here in

---

* George W. Cutting Jr. played a large role in the life of Weston for
decades. He owned the general store at the center of town and held many
offices, including clerk.

† Benjamin Loring Young gave the opening address at the dedication.
Young served as a Weston selectman and a state representative.

‡ The Battles of Lexington and Concord, igniting the Revolutionary War,
occurred on April 19, 1775.

this town leading up to that great day. General Gage was in command of the British forces at Boston.* There had been gathered supplies for carrying on a war out here through Middlesex County and out to the west in Worcester. History tells us that he sent out here Sergeant Howe and other spies,† in order that he might find out what the conditions were and whether it would be easy for the British troops to come out here and seize those supplies and break what they thought was the idea on the part of the colonists of starting a rebellion. Sergeant Howe came out here, went to the hotel, where, of course, the landlord received him hospitably, but informed him that probably it wouldn't be a healthy place for him to stay for a very long time, and sent him away in the dead of the night. He went back to Boston and made a report to the General in which he said that the people of this vicinity were generally resolved to be free or to die. That was the spirit of those times; and he advised the Britishers that if they wanted to go out to Worcester they would probably need an expedition of ten thousand men and a sufficient train of artillery, and

---

* At the start of the Revolution, General Thomas Gage served as military governor of Massachusetts and commander of British forces in North America.

† In 1827, a printer named Luther Roby published *The Journal Kept by Mr. John Howe While He Was Employed as a British Spy; Also, While He Was Engaged in the Smuggling Business.* For more than 150 years, historians treated it as a true account. In 1993, however, historian Daniel E. Williams revealed the journal — and Howe — to be a fabrication. General Gage did send out men to gather information, but the fictitious Howe did not rank among them.

he doubted whether, if such an expedition as that were sent out, any part of it would return alive. On account of the report that he brought back it was determined by the British authorities that it was more prudent to go up to Concord than it was to come out here on the way to Worcester. That was the reason that the expedition on that Nineteenth of April was started for Concord rather than through here for Worcester.

Of course, there are many other interesting events in the history of this town. You had here many men who have seen military service. You furnished a large number for the Revolutionary War and a large amount of money. You furnished as your quota one hundred and twenty-six soldiers that went into the army from 1861 to 1865. But you were doing here what they were doing all over the Commonwealth of Massachusetts. I doubt if the leading and prominent and decisive part that Massachusetts played in the great Revolutionary War is generally understood. It is interesting to recall that when General Washington came here he seems to have come with somewhat of a prejudice against New England men. I think there are extant letters which he wrote at that time rather reflecting upon what the New England men were doing and the character of Massachusetts men of those days.* But that was not his idea at the end of the

---

* General Washington expressed his disappointment in the troops and arms he encountered when he arrived in Boston in July 1775, Washington reported to the Continental Congress on the "Deficiency of Numbers, Discipline & Stores"

war. Then, although he had been brought up far to the south, he had a different idea. Then he said, and said very generously, that he thought well of New England men and had it not been for their support, had it not been for the men, the materials and munitions that they supplied to the Revolutionary forces, the war would not have been a success. His name is interestingly connected with your town of Weston.

You have had here not only an interesting population but an interesting location. It was through this town that the great arteries of travel ran to the west and south and to the north. When Burgoyne surrendered, some of his troops were brought through this town on their way to the sea-coast.* When Washington came up to visit New England after he had been President, he came through the town of Weston, and I do not know whether this is any reflection on the cooking of those days in the towns to the west, but it says in the history of the town of Weston that at one time when Washington stopped at the hotel in Wayland, although the hostess

---

he observed. The next month, Washington confided in a letter to his cousin that the officers of the New England army "generally speaking are the most indifferent kind of People I ever saw." He added, "I daresay the Men would fight very well (if properly Officered) although they are an exceeding dirty & nasty people."

* On October 17, 1777, British general John Burgoyne surrendered to American general Horatio Gates at Saratoga. The battle marked a turning point in the Revolutionary War. The Americans marched Burgoyne's nearly six thousand troops to Cambridge, Massachusetts, where they went into captivity.

had provided what she thought was a very fine banquet, he left his staff to eat that and went out into the kitchen to help himself to a bowl of bread and milk. I suppose he would not be thought to have done that because he was a candidate for office and wanted to appear as one of the plain people, because that was after he had served in the office of President. But he stopped here in the town of Weston and was entertained here at the hotel. And many other great men passed through here and were entertained here from the time when we were colonies clear up to the time when the railroads were established along in the middle of the last century.

So this town has had a long and interesting history, and has done its part in building up Massachusetts and giving her strength to take her part in the history of this great Nation. And it is pleasant to see how the work that the fathers have done before us is bearing fruit in these times of ours. It is interesting to see this beautiful building. It is interesting to know that you have a town planning committee who are placing this building in a situation where it will contribute to the physical beauty of this historic town. We have not given the time and the attention and the thought that we should have given to things of that kind in Massachusetts. We have been too utilitarian. We have thought that if a building was located in some place where we could have access to it, where it could be used, where it could transact the business of the town, that was enough. We are coming to

see in these modern days that that is not enough; that
we need not only utilitarian motives, but that we need to
give some time, some thought and attention to the artis-
tic in life; that we need to concern ourselves not only
with the material but give some thought to the spiritual;
that we need to pay some attention to the beautiful as
well as to that which is merely useful.

These things are appreciated. Weston is doing something along these lines and building her public buildings and laying out her public square or her common
(as it was known in the old days) so they will be things
of beauty as well as things of use. Let us dedicate this
building to these new purposes. Let us dedicate it to
the glorious history of the past. Let us dedicate it to the
sacrifice that is required in these present days. Let us
dedicate it to the hope of the future. Let us dedicate it
to New England ideals — those ideals that have made
Massachusetts one of the strong States of the Nation;
strong enough so that in Revolutionary days we contributed far in excess of our portion of men and money
to that great struggle; strong enough so that the whole
Nation has looked to Massachusetts in days of stress for
comfort and support.

We are very proud of our democracy. We are very
proud of our form of government. We believe that there
is no other nation on earth that gives to the individual
the privileges and the rights that he has in America.
The time has come now when we are going to defend

those rights. The time has come when the world is looking to America, as the Nation has looked to Massachusetts in the past, to stand up and defend the rights of the individual. Sovereignty, it is our belief, is vested in the individual; and we are going to protect the rights of the individual. It is an auspicious moment to dedicate here in New England one of our town halls, an auspicious moment in which to dedicate it to the supremacy of those ideals for which the whole world is fighting at the present time; that the rights of the individual as they were established here in the past may be maintained by us now and carried to a yet greater development in the future.

XV

AMHERST ALUMNI DINNER, SPRINGFIELD

MARCH 15, 1918

"Without the support of the moral power of
the Nation armies will prove useless."

In 1918, Governor Samuel McCall decided not to seek reelection and instead to run for U.S. Senate. This decision opened the way for Coolidge. In that campaign year, Coolidge again addressed his fellow Amherst alumni, a group whose support would prove key to his national career — classmate Dwight Morrow would lobby tirelessly for Coolidge at the 1920 Republican National Convention. During this dinner speech, Coolidge reflects on the "moral power" needed for America to prevail in the Great War.

The individual may not require the higher institutions of learning, but society does. Without them civilization as we know it would fall from mankind in a night. They minister not alone to their own students, they minister to all humanity.

It is this same ancient spirit which, coming to the defence of the Nation, has in this new day of peril made nearly every college campus a training field for military service, and again sent graduate and undergraduate into the fighting forces of our country.* They are demonstrating again that they are the strongholds of ordered liberty and individual freedom. This has ever been the distinguishing characteristic of the American institution of learning. They have believed in democracy because they believed in the nobility of man; they have served society because they have looked upon the possession of learning not as conferring a privilege but as laying on a duty. They have taught and practised the precept that the greater man's power the greater his obligation. The supreme choice is righteousness. It is that "moral power" to which Professor Tyler referred as the great contribution of college men to the cause of the Union.†

---

* In Amherst's case, a third of the student body withdrew from school as soon as the United States declared war. By graduation a couple of months later, only thirty-five seniors remained on campus.

† Professor William Seymour Tyler taught Greek at Amherst. In a long essay titled "Prayer for Colleges," Tyler wrote about "moral power" and the responsibilities of college-educated men as leaders and thinkers. According to the Amherst Historical Commission, Tyler gave a "rousing sermon in the chapel of the college" when the Civil War began. "One hundred students gave their names to enlist immediately afterwards."

The Nation is taking a military census, it is thinking now in terms of armament. The officers of government are discussing manpower, transportation by land and sea and through the air, the production of rifles, artillery, and explosives, the raising of money by loans and taxation. The Nation ought to be most mightily engaged in this work. It must put every ounce of its resources into the production and organization of its material power. But these are to a degree but the outward manifestations of something yet more important. The ultimate result of all wars and of this war has been and will be determined by the moral power of the nations engaged. On that will depend whether armies "ray out darkness" or are the source of light and life and liberty. Without the support of the moral power of the Nation armies will prove useless, without a moral victory, whatever the fortunes of the battlefield, there can be no abiding peace.

Whatever the difficulties of an exact definition may be the manifestations of moral power are not difficult to recognize. The life of America is rich with such examples. It has been predominant here. It established thirteen colonies which were to a large degree self-sustaining and self-governing. They fought and won a revolutionary war. What manner of men they were, what was the character of their leadership, was attested only in part by Saratoga and Yorktown. Washington had displayed great power on many fields of battle, the colonists had suffered long and endured to the end, but the glory of military power fades away beside the picture of the victorious general, returning his commission to the representatives of a people who would have made him king, and retiring after two terms from the Presidency which he could have held for life, and the picture of a war-worn people turning from debt, disorder, almost anarchy, not to division, not to despotism, but to national unity under the ordered liberty of the Federal Constitution.

It was manifested again in the adoption and defence by the young nation of that principle which is known as the Monroe Doctrine that European despotism should make no further progress in the Western Hemisphere. It is in the great argument of Webster replying to Hayne and the stout declaration of Jackson that he would treat nullification as treason.* It was the compelling force of the Civil War, expounded by Lincoln in his unyielding purpose to save the Union but "with malice toward none, with charity for all,"† which General Grant, his greatest soldier, put into practice at Appomattox when he sent General Lee back with his sword, and his soldiers

---

* Coolidge refers to the nullification crisis of the early 1830s. In January 1830, Senator Robert Hayne of South Carolina argued that states could nullify federal law. In response, Senator Daniel Webster of Massachusetts gave the famous oration in which he declared, "Liberty and Union, now and forever, one and inseparable!" (Coolidge also cited this speech during his July 4, 1916, address at Daniel Webster's home [see page 30].) In 1832, President Andrew Jackson and Vice President John C. Calhoun split over nullification. Calhoun resigned the vice presidency and entered the Senate — filling Robert Hayne's seat, as it happened.

† The famous peroration of Lincoln's second inaugural address.

home to the plantations, with their war horses for the spring plowing. And at the conclusion of the Spanish War it is to the ever-enduring credit of our country that it exacted not penalties, but justice, and actually compensated a defeated foe for public property that had come to our hands in the Philippines as the result of the fortunes of battle.* But what of the present crisis? Is the heart of the Nation still sound, does it still respond to the appeal to the high ideals of the past? If those two and one half years, before the American declaration of war, shall appear, when unprejudiced history is written, to have been characterized by patience, forbearance, and self-restraint, they will add to the credit of former days. If they were characterized by selfishness, by politics, by a balancing of expediency against justice they will be counted as a time of ignominy for which a victorious war would furnish scant compensation.

---

* At the end of the Spanish-American War, in 1898, Spain ceded the Philippines to the United States for $20 million. The U.S. Senate ratified the peace treaty by only one vote, reflecting concerns about American imperialism.

XVI

MESSAGE FOR THE *BOSTON POST*

APRIL 22, 1918

"Have faith in the moral power of America."

Returning to the theme of his Amherst alumni speech, Coolidge discusses moral power in this letter to the Boston Post.

The nation with the greatest moral power will win. Of that are born armies and navies and the resolution to endure. Have faith in the moral power of America. It gave independence under Washington and freedom under Lincoln. Here, right never lost. Here, wrong never won. However powerful the forces of evil may appear, somewhere there are more powerful forces of righteousness. Courage and confidence are our heritage. Justice is our might. The outcome is in your hand, my fellow American; if you deserve to win, the Nation cannot lose.

XVII

ROXBURY HISTORICAL SOCIETY, BUNKER HILL DAY

JUNE 17, 1918

"The law of progress and civilization is not the law of the jungle. It is not an earthly law, it is a divine law."

A common Coolidge caricature shows him focused only on material success. Yet he often emphasized that, as he would put it in 1926, "the things of the spirit come first." In this speech, Coolidge ties the sacrifices Americans made at the Battle of Bunker Hill to the sacrifices necessary in the Great War.

Reverence is the measure not of others but of ourselves. This assemblage on the one hundred and forty-third anniversary of the Battle of Bunker Hill tells not only of the spirit of that day but of the spirit of to-day. What men worship that will they become. The heroes and holidays of a people which fascinate their soul reveal what they hold are the realities of life and mark out a line beyond which they will not retreat, but at which they will stand to overcome or die. They who reverence Bunker Hill will fight there. Your true patriot sees home and hearthstone in the welfare of his country.

Rightly viewed, then, this day is set apart for an examination of ourselves by recounting the deeds of the men of long ago. What was there in the events of the seventeenth day of June, 1775, which holds the veneration of Americans and the increasing admiration of the world? There are the physical facts not too unimportant to be unworthy of reiteration even in the learned presence of an Historical Society. A detachment of men clad for the most part in the dress of their daily occupations, standing with bared heads and muskets grounded muzzle down in the twilight glow on Cambridge Common, heard Samuel Langdon, President of Harvard College,* seek divine blessing on their cause and marched away in the darkness to a little eminence at Charlestown, where, ere the setting of another sun, much history was to be made and much glory lost and won. When a new dawn had lifted the mists of the Bay, the British, under General Howe,† saw an intrenchment

---

* After the Revolutionary War began, Harvard housed troops in four of its buildings. The Reverend Samuel Langdon, Harvard's president, prayed over the soldiers before the Battle of Bunker Hill.

† General William Howe led the British troops at Bunker Hill. Soon he would take command of British land forces in North America.

on Breed's Hill,* which must be taken or Boston abandoned. The works were exposed in the rear to attack from land and sea. This was disdained by the king's soldiers in their contempt for the supposed fighting ability of the Americans. Leisurely, as on dress parade, they assembled for an assault that they thought was to be a demonstration of the uselessness of any armed resistance on the part of the Colonies. In splendid array they advanced late in the day. A few straggling shots and all was still behind the parapet. It was easier than they had expected. But when they reached a point where 't is said the men behind the intrenchments could see the whites of their eyes,† they were met by a withering fire that tore their ranks asunder and sent them back in disorder, utterly routed by their despised foes. In time they form and advance again but the result is the same. The demonstration of superiority was not a success. For a third time they form, not now for dress parade, but for a hazardous assault. This time the result was different. The patriots had lost nothing of courage or determination but there was left scarcely one round of powder. They had no bayonets. Pouring in their last volley and

---

* The Americans had been ordered to fortify Bunker Hill, but, marching in the dark, they moved past that hill and instead began fortifying a smaller elevation nearby, Breed's Hill. Most of the fighting occurred on Breed's Hill. The Bunker Hill Monument stands on Breed's Hill.

† Coolidge refers to the famous command "Don't fire till you see the whites of their eyes," often attributed to either Colonel William Prescott or Colonel Israel Putnam.

still resisting with clubbed muskets, they retired slowly and in order from the field. So great was the British loss that there was no pursuit. The intensity of the battle is told by the loss of the Americans, out of about fifteen hundred engaged, of nearly twenty per cent, and of the British, out of some thirty-five hundred engaged, of nearly thirty-three per cent, all in one and one half hours.*

It was the story of brave men bravely led but insufficiently equipped. Their leader, Colonel Prescott, had walked the breastworks to show his men that the cannonade was not particularly dangerous. John Stark, bringing his company, in which were his Irish compatriots, across Charlestown Neck under the guns of the battleships, refused to quicken his step. His Major, Andrew McCleary, fell at the rail fence which he had held during the day. Dr. Joseph Warren, your own son of Roxbury, fell in the retreat, but the Americans, though picking off his officers, spared General Howe. They had fought the French under his brother.†

Such were some of the outstanding deeds of the

---

* The Americans lost the Battle of Bunker Hill. Yet, as Coolidge suggests, the high casualty rate showed the British that they faced a difficult fight against the colonies. The battle also boosted the Americans' confidence.

† Brigadier General George Howe was, in the words of one historian, "the most beloved British regular officer to serve in the colonies during the French and Indian War." Americans mourned when George Howe was killed in battle in 1758. A third brother, Admiral Richard Howe, commanded British naval troops in the Revolutionary War.

day. But these were the deeds of men and the deeds of men always have an inward significance. In distant Philadelphia, on this very day, the Continental Congress had chosen as the Commander of their Army, General George Washington, a man whose clear vision looked into the realities of things and did not falter. On his way to the front four days later, dispatches reached him of the battle. He revealed the meaning of the day with one question, "Did the militia fight?" Learning how those heroic men fought, he said, "Then the liberties of the Country are safe." No greater commentary has ever been made on the significance of Bunker Hill.

We read events by what goes before and after. We think of Bunker Hill as the first real battle for independence, the prelude to the Revolution. Yet these were both afterthoughts. Independence Day was still more than a year away and then eight years from accomplishment. The Revolution cannot be said to have become established until the adoption of the Federal Constitution. No, on this June day, these were not the conscious objects sought. They were contending for the liberties of the country, they were not yet bent on establishing a new nation nor on recognizing that relationship between men which the modern world calls democracy. They were maintaining well their traditions, these sons of Londonderry, lovers of freedom and anxious for the fray, and these sons of the Puritans, whom Macaulay tells us humbly abased themselves in the dust before the

Lord, but hesitated not to set their foot upon the neck of their king.*

It is the moral quality of the day that abides. It was the purpose of those plain garbed men behind the parapet that told whether they were savages bent on plunder, living under the law of the jungle, or sons of the morning bearing the light of civilization. The glorious revolution of 1688 was fading from memory.† The English Government of that day rested upon privilege and corruption at the base, surmounted by a king bent on despotism, but fortunately too weak to accomplish any design either of good or ill.‡ An empire still outwardly sound was rotting at the core. The privilege which had found Great Britain so complacent sought to establish itself over the Colonies. The purpose of the patriots was resistance to tyranny. Pitt and Burke and Lord Camden in England recognized this, and, loving liberty, approved

---

* The historian Thomas Babington Macaulay, in his 1825 "Essay on Milton," wrote that "the Puritan was made up of two different men, the one all self-abasement, penitence, gratitude, passion, the other proud, calm, inflexible, sagacious." The Puritan, Macaulay wrote, "prostrated himself in the dust before his Maker: but he set his foot on the neck of his king."

† In the Glorious Revolution, Parliament gained new powers over the British monarchy. King James II fled England after William of Orange, the Dutch husband of James's daughter Mary, invaded. Parliament recognized William and Mary as king and queen when the pair signed a Declaration of Rights and accepted new restrictions on the power of the crown.

‡ The king in question, George III, was the target of the Founders' grievances in the Declaration of Independence. In *Common Sense* (1776), Thomas Paine called King George III "the Royal Brute of Great Britain."

the course of the Colonies.* The Tories here, loving
privilege, approved the course of the Royal Government.
Bunker Hill meant that the Colonies would save themselves and saving themselves save the mother country
for liberty. The war was not inevitable. Perhaps wars are
never inevitable. But the conflict between freedom and
privilege was inevitable. That it broke out in America
rather than in England was accidental. Liberty, the rights
of man against tyranny, the rights of kings, was in the
air. One side must give way. There might have been a
peaceful settlement by timely concessions such as the
Reform Bill of England some fifty years later, or the
Japanese reforms of our own times,† but wanting that
a collision was inevitable. Lacking a Bunker Hill there
had been another Dunbar.‡

The eighteenth century was the era of the development of political rights. It was the culmination of the
ideas of the Renaissance. It was the putting into practice
in government of the answer to the long pondered and
much discussed question, "What is right?" Custom was

---

* William Pitt the Elder, Edmund Burke, and Charles Pratt, 1st Earl Camden,
all challenged Britain's policies toward the American colonies.

† England's First Reform Act, passed in 1832, overhauled the nation's anti-
quated electoral system and extended voting rights to new groups. Beginning
in 1912, under the Taisho emperor, Japan expanded the vote and modernized
its economy. These reforms continued a transformation that had begun under
Taisho's father during the Meiji Restoration.

‡ At the Battle of Dunbar in 1650, English forces under Oliver Cromwell
defeated the Scots to preempt a Scottish invasion.

giving way at last to reason. Class and caste and place, all the distinctions based on appearance and accident were giving way before reality. Men turned from distinctions which were temporal to those which were eternal. The sovereignty of kings and the nobility of peers was swallowed up in the sovereignty and nobility of all men. The inequal in quantity became equal in quality.

The successful solution of this problem was the crowning glory of a century and a half of America. It established for all time how men ought to act toward each other in the governmental relation. The rule of the people had begun.

Bunker Hill had a deeper significance. It was an example of the great law of human progress and civilization. There has been much talk in recent years of the survival of the fittest and of efficiency. We are beginning to hear of the development of the super-man and the claim that he has of right dominion over the rest of his inferiors on earth.* This philosophy denies the doctrine of equality and holds that government is not based on consent but on compulsion. It holds that the weak must serve the strong, which is the law of slavery, it applies the law of the animal world to mankind and

---

* The German philosopher Friedrich Nietzsche had developed the concept of the *Übermensch* in his 1883 book, *Thus Spoke Zarathustra*. The first English translation appeared in 1896, and the first to translate *Übermensch* as "Superman" appeared in 1909. The idea of a superman leader carried over into national politics.

puts science above morals. This sounds the call to the jungle. It is not an advance to the morning but a retreat to night. It is not the light of human reason but the darkness of the wisdom of the serpent.

The law of progress and civilization is not the law of the jungle. It is not an earthly law, it is a divine law. It does not mean the survival of the fittest, it means the sacrifice of the fittest. Any mother will give her life for her child. Men put the women and children in the lifeboats before they themselves will leave the sinking ship. John Hampden and Nathan Hale did not survive,* nor did Lincoln, but Benedict Arnold did. The example above all others takes us back to Jerusalem some nineteen hundred years ago. The men of Bunker Hill were true disciples of civilization, because they were willing to sacrifice themselves to resist the evils and redeem the liberties of the British Empire. The proud shaft which rises over their battlefield and the bronze form of Joseph Warren in your square are not monuments to expediency or success, they are monuments to righteousness.

This is the age-old story. Men are reading it again to-day — written in blood. The Prussian military

---

* John Hampden was one of the five members of Parliament whom King Charles I attempted to arrest in 1642, an event that helped spark the First English Civil War. In 1643, Hampden died after being wounded at the Battle of Chalgrove Field. Nathan Hale answered George Washington's call for spies to go behind British lines. Captured, he was hanged on September 22, 1776. Legend holds that Hale's last words were "I only regret that I have but one life to lose for my country."

despotism has abandoned the law of civilization for the law of barbarism. We could approve, and join in the scramble to the jungle, or we could resist and sacrifice ourselves to save an erring nation. Not being beasts, but men, we choose the sacrifice.

This brings us to the part that America is taking at the end of its second hundred and fifty years of existence. Is it not a part of that increasing purpose which the poet, the seer, tells us runs through the ages? Has not our Nation been raised up and strengthened, trained and prepared, to meet the great sacrifice that must be made now to save the world from despotism?* We have heard much of our lack of preparation. We have been altogether lacking in preparation in a strict military sense. We had no vast forces of artillery or infantry, no large stores of munitions, few trained men. But let us not forget to pay proper respect to the preparation we did have, which was the result of long training and careful teaching. We had a mental, a moral, a spiritual training that fitted us equally with any other people to engage in this great contest which after all is a contest of ideas as well as of arms. We must never neglect the military preparation again, but we may as well recognize that we have had a preparation without which arms in

---

* When, on April 2, 1917, President Woodrow Wilson had called for a declaration of war on Germany, he said that "the world must be made safe for democracy" and that America "must bring peace and safety to all nations and make the world itself at last free."

our hands would very much resemble in purpose those now arrayed against us.

Are we not realizing a noble destiny? The great Admiral who discovered America bore the significant name of Christopher. It has been pointed out that this name means Christ-bearer. Were not the men who stood at Bunker Hill bearing light to the world by their sacrifices? Are not the men of to-day, the entire Nation of to-day, living in accordance with the significance of that name, and by their service and sacrifice redeeming mankind from the forces that make for everlasting destruction? We seek no territory and no rewards. We give but do not take. We seek for a victory of our ideas. Our arms are but the means. America follows no such delusion as a place in the sun for the strong by the destruction of the weak. America seeks rather, by giving of her strength for the service of the weak, a place in eternity.

XVIII

FAIRHAVEN

JULY 4, 1918

"Here was a youth who determined to pursue the
course which he had been taught was right."

*In 1841, a whaling ship captained by William H. Whitfield
of Fairhaven, Massachusetts, came upon five Japanese fishermen on the uninhabited island of Tori-shima. Captain Whitfield brought the fishermen to safety in Honolulu, but one,
a fourteen-year-old named Manjirō, begged to stay with him.
Captain Whitfield brought him back to Fairhaven, making
Manjirō one of the first Japanese to come to the United
States. In the 1850s, after Manjirō returned to Japan, he
became an important interpreter when Commodore Matthew
Perry arrived to open Japan to trade. Japan's shogunate government made Manjirō a samurai.*

*On July 4, 1918, Lieutenant Governor Coolidge traveled
to Fairhaven to welcome Japanese diplomat Ishii Kikujirō,*

who presented the town with a samurai sword (rendered here
as "Sumari sword") on behalf of Manjirō's son. The respect
Coolidge shows here for Japan, and Japanese dignity, would
appear again when President Coolidge deplored the Japanese
exclusion in the 1924 Immigration Act.

We have met on this anniversary of American independence to assess the dimensions of a kind deed. Nearly four score years ago the master of a whaling vessel sailing from this port rescued from a barren rock in the China Sea some Japanese fishermen. Among them was a young boy whom he brought home with him to Fairhaven, where he was given the advantages of New England life and sent to school with the boys and girls of the neighborhood, where he excelled in his studies. But as he grew up he was filled with a longing to see Japan and his aged mother. He knew that the duty of filial piety lay upon him according to the teachings of his race, and he was determined to meet that obligation. I think that is one of the lessons of this day. Here was a youth who determined to pursue the course which he had been taught was right. He braved the dangers of the voyage and the greater dangers that awaited an absentee from his country under the then existing laws, to perform his duty to his mother and to his native land. In making that return I think we are entitled to say that he was the first Ambassador of America to the Court of Japan, for his extraordinary experience soon brought

HIS FIRST POLITICAL EXPERIENCE. As a boy in isolated Plymouth Notch, Vermont, Calvin Coolidge learned politics at the town meeting, where he sold apples and watched the debates. Civility and compromise proved key to passing any town resolution. Calvin's father, John, served as a bailiff and justice of the peace.

THE AMHERST NETWORK. At Amherst College, Coolidge debated national issues with classmates and made the acquaintance of students who would later prove strong allies in politics. One was Dwight Morrow, who at first underestimated Coolidge but grew to appreciate his depth, integrity, and potential. Morrow later wrote a letter to fellow Amherst alumnus Frank Stearns in which he said: "Calvin is one of the fellows who is real. He really wants to make things better, not to pretend to make them better." Coolidge also attended Amherst with Harlan Fiske Stone. President Coolidge would later tap Stone for U.S. attorney general and then Supreme Court justice.

NORTHAMPTON NETWORK. John Hammond and Henry Field, Coolidge's first employers after he graduated from Amherst, were active in Massachusetts state politics. While clerking at their law firm in the city of Northampton, Coolidge took in the rudiments of party politics. In the era before autos, attorneys often walked to meet their clients — and candidates walked to meet constituents. Voters learned to appreciate the quiet young man, and he, them. Coolidge told his fellow citizens: "I want your vote. I need it. I shall appreciate it."

"I HAVE REJOICED IN HER GRACES." Coolidge entered politics early, rising from city councilman to state representative to Northampton mayor to state senator. In 1905 the bachelor's life transformed when he married Grace Anna Goodhue, a graduate of a teaching program at the Clarke School for the Deaf. Grace's mother had suggested the pair wait a year before marrying while Grace learned to bake bread and keep house. "We can buy bread," Coolidge snapped, and the wedding took place without delay. Sons John (born 1906) and Calvin Jr. (1908) completed the family.

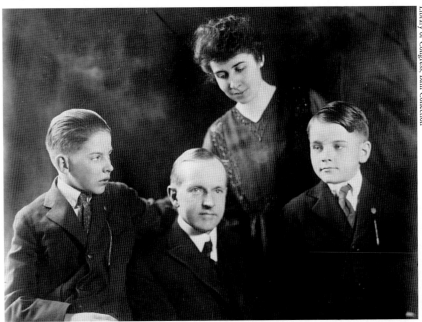

A COMMON INTEREST. The 1912 Bread and Roses Strike by textile workers in Lawrence, Massachusetts, gave Coolidge, then a state senator, some of his first experience mediating between employers and workers. Coolidge chaired a special government committee that helped settle the strike and subsequently secured passage of a mothers' aid bill. The Bread and Roses experience taught Coolidge that capital and labor have a common interest. Coolidge, however, also reached another conclusion: that some of the strikers sought not compromise but rather to "destroy all authority."

"AMERICANISM." Throughout his career in Massachusetts politics, Coolidge reminded Bay State citizens of their history. *At right:* Coolidge leaves the historic home of Daniel Webster, the famed nineteenth-century orator and statesman. Coolidge gave a rousing speech at the Webster home on July 4, 1916 (*see page 23*).

"A PEOPLE WHO HAVE NEVER FAILED TO RESPOND TO AN ACT OF KINDNESS." Even as a Massachusetts politician, Coolidge believed in the importance of diplomatic effort toward Japan. Lieutenant Governor Coolidge underscored this point on July 4, 1918, when Japanese dignitaries visited Massachusetts. That day, Coolidge spoke at the historic home of Captain William H. Whitfield, who in the 1840s rescued Japanese fishermen marooned on an uninhabited Pacific island. One of the fishermen, a fourteen-year-old named Manjirō, asked to come live with Whitfield in Massachusetts, at a time when Japan was closed to the world. Manjirō (*left*) later returned to Japan and became an important interpreter when Commodore Matthew Perry arrived to open Japan to trade. Coolidge praised Manjirō as "the first Ambassador of America to the Court of Japan." When, as president, Coolidge signed a restrictive immigration law, he deplored a section in the law banning Japanese immigration to the United States.

"HAVE FAITH IN MASSACHUSETTS." By the time Coolidge became Massachusetts governor (*right*), he had more than twenty years' experience in politics. The young lawmaker at first backed progressive legislation. Over time, however, Coolidge came to question the pace of reform and the proliferation of legislation. When his own father became a state lawmaker in Vermont, Coolidge wrote a word of counsel: "It is much more important to kill bad bills than to pass good ones."

CRUCIAL MENTORS. Coolidge's political mentor in Massachusetts was U.S. senator Winthrop Murray Crane (*above left*). Crane headed his family's paper company, still known today for its stationery. Crane's silent — and successful — style made an impression on Coolidge. Later, Coolidge called Crane "the most disinterested public servant I ever saw and the greatest influence for good government with which I ever came in contact." Crane died in 1920, shortly before Coolidge was elected vice president. A second mentor to Coolidge, as well as a financial supporter, emerged in Amherst alumnus and department store proprietor Frank Stearns (*above right*). Stearns spearheaded the publication of the first edition of *Have Faith in Massachusetts*.

"HIS ACTS WERE PROMPTED BY HIGH MOTIVES." As governor of one of the states welcoming returning servicemen after the war, Coolidge encountered foreign policy firsthand. In 1919, Governor Coolidge hosted President Woodrow Wilson upon the president's return from negotiating the Versailles Treaty in France. Coolidge's appreciation for Wilson's efforts in international diplomacy would later show up in his own stewardship of the 1928 Kellogg-Briand Pact, which outlawed war as a means of settling international disputes.

THE TEST OF THE STRIKE. The great test of Coolidge's career came just two months before he ran for reelection as governor. In September 1919, the Boston police force broke its contract and walked out on strike. (*Above*, policemen carry away their belongings the first night of the strike.) In unpoliced Boston, riots and mayhem ensued (*below*). Coolidge faced pressure to compromise with the police union. Instead, the governor authorized the police commissioner to fire the striking officers.

"THERE IS NO RIGHT TO STRIKE..." Governor Coolidge called out the state guard (*above*, pictured on the roof of Boston's Faneuil Hall). Through American Federation of Labor leader Samuel Gompers, the police sought compromise and reinstatement. But in a telegraph to Gompers, Coolidge declared, "There is no right to strike against the public safety by anybody, anywhere, any time." This categoric statement resonated with Americans weary of violence. It made Coolidge a national figure.

NOTIFICATION DAY. The original edition of *Have Faith in Massachusetts* was nearly complete when the Boston police strike put Coolidge on the national stage. Supporter Frank Stearns rushed the book into print to get it in the hands of delegates to the Republican National Convention, to be held the following summer. At the convention, a delegate who had read and admired the book nominated Coolidge for vice president. The *Boston Globe* called Coolidge's nomination "the first real, wholly unpremeditated stampede that ever took place at a national convention." *Above:* Friends old and new rallied around Coolidge when he received the vice-presidential nomination. Here, Coolidge shakes hands with the legendary Henry Cabot Lodge, senior senator from Massachusetts. To the left of Coolidge stands the junior senator, Murray Crane.

NORMALCY. In 1920, Americans hungered for a return to prewar calm. Senator Warren Harding of Ohio won the first place on the Republican presidential ticket, with Coolidge as his running mate. The pair won the 1920 election on a program they called "normalcy." Harding and Coolidge promised to restore stable conditions that would enable America to move past crisis — including less intrusive taxation, less regulation, and the rule of law. "Our best assurance," Harding said in his inaugural address, "lies in efficient administration of our proven system."

him into the association of the highest officials of his
country, and his presence there prepared the way for the
friendly reception which was given to Commodore Perry
when he was sent to Japan to open relations between
that Government and the Government of America.

And so we see how out of the kind deed of Captain
Whitefield,* friendly relations which have existed for
many years between the people of Japan and the people
of America were encouraged and made possible. And it
is in recognition of that event that we have here to-day
this great concourse of people, this martial array, and the
representative of the Japanese people — a people who
have never failed to respond to an act of kindness.

It was with special pleasure that I came here representing the Commonwealth of Massachusetts, to extend
an official welcome to His Excellency Viscount Ishii,
who comes here to present to the town of Fairhaven a
Sumari sword on behalf of the son of that boy who was
rescued long ago. This sword was once the emblem of
place and caste and arbitrary rank. It has taken on a new
significance because Captain Whitefield was true to the
call of humanity, because a Japanese boy was true to his
call of duty. This emblem will hereafter be a token not
only of the friendship that exists between two nations
but a token of liberty, of freedom, and of the recognition

---

* William H. Whitfield — the original edition misspelled the captain's
name.

by the Government of both these nations of the rights of the people. Let it remain here as a mutual pledge by the giver and the receiver of their determination that the motive which inspired the representatives of each race to do right is to be a motive which is to govern the people of the earth.

XIX

SOMERVILLE REPUBLICAN CITY COMMITTEE

AUGUST 7, 1918

"The only hope of a short war is
to prepare for a long one."

*Coolidge was running for governor in 1918, but with the
nation at war, he put country above party. In this speech, he
calls on Americans to sacrifice. He also addresses an issue
few politicians of the day did: racial justice. His praise for
African American soldiers echoes points he later made as
president, including his comment "If all men are created
equal, that is final."*

C oming into your presence in ordinary times, gentlemen of the committee, I should be inclined to
direct your attention to the long and patriotic services
of our party, to the great benefits its policies have conferred upon this Nation, to the illustrious names of our

leaders, to our present activities, and to our future party policy. But these are not ordinary times. Our country is at war. There is no way to save our party if our country be lost. And in the present crisis there is only one way to save our country. We must support the State and National Governments in whatever they request for the conduct of the war. The Constitution makes the President Commander-in-Chief of the Army and Navy. What he needs should be freely given. This has been and will be the policy of the Republican administration of Massachusetts and of her Senators and Representatives in Congress. We seek no party advantage from the distress of our country. Among Republicans there will be no political profiteering.

It is a year and four months now since we declared the German Government was making war on America. We are beginning to see what our requirements are. We had a small but efficient standing army, and a larger but less efficient National Guard. These have been increased by enlistments. We have a new national force, — never to be designated as Conscripts, but as the accepted soldiers of a whole Nation that has volunteered, of almost unlimited numbers. By taxation and by three Liberty Loans, each over-subscribed by more than fifty per cent, we have demonstrated that there will be no lack of money. The problem of the production and conservation of food is being met, though not yet without some inconvenience, yet so far with very little suffering.

The remaining factor is the production of the necessary materials for carrying on the war. We lack ships and military supplies. Whether these are secured in time in sufficient quantity will depend in a large measure upon the attitude of the people managing and employed in these industries. The attitude of the leaders of organized labor has been patriotic. They realize that this is a war to preserve the rights that have been won for the people, and they have at all times advised their fellow workmen to remain at work. There must be forbearance on all sides. Where wages are too low they should be increased voluntarily. Where there is disagreement the Government has provided means for investigation and adjustment. Our industrial front must keep pace with our military front.

We are demonstrating the ability of America. Within the last few days the report has come to us that our soldiers have defeated the Prussian Guard. The sneer of Germany at America is vanishing. It is true that the German high command still couple American and African soldiers together in intended derision. What they say in scorn, let us say in praise. We have fought before for the rights of all men irrespective of color. We are proud to fight now with colored men for the rights of white men. It would be fitting recognition of their worth to send our American negro, when that time comes, to inform the Prussian military despotism on what terms their defeated armies are to be granted peace.

While the victories that have recently come to our arms are most encouraging, they should only stimulate us to redoubled efforts. The only hope of a short war is to prepare for a long one. In this work the States play a most important part. Massachusetts must be kept so organized and governed as to continue that able, effective, and prompt coöperation with the National Government that has marked the past progress of the war. In this we have a great part to do here. It was for such a task that the Republican Party came into being sixty-four years ago. One of the resolutions adopted at its birth peculiarly dedicates it to the requirements of the present hour.

"Resolved, that in view of the necessity of battling for the first principles of republican government and against the schemes of an aristocracy, the most revolting and oppressive with which the earth was ever cursed, or man debased, we will coöperate and be known as 'Republicans' until the contest be terminated."*

This great work lies before our party in Massachusetts. We shall go on battling for the first principles of Republican government until it has been secured to all the people of the earth.

---

* The Republican Party was born in explicit opposition to slavery. On July 6, 1854, some ten thousand people attended the meeting in Jackson, Michigan, at which the Republicans adopted a platform that included the resolution Coolidge quotes here. The platform also condemned slavery as "a great moral, social, and political evil."

Our American forces on sea and land are proving sufficient to turn the tide in favor of the Allied cause. They could not succeed alone, we could not succeed alone. We are furnishing a reserve power that is bringing victory.

But America must furnish more than armies and navies for the future. If armies and navies were to be supreme, Germany would be right. There are other and greater forces in the world than march to the roll of the drum. As we are turning the scale with our sword now, so hereafter we must turn the scale with the moral power of America. It must be our disinterested plans that are to restore Europe to a place through justice when we have secured victory through the sword.* And into a new world we are to take not only the people of oppressed Europe but the people of America. Out of our sacrifice and suffering, out of our blood and tears, America shall have a new awakening, a rededication to the cause of Washington and Lincoln, a firmer conviction for the right.

---

* In the event, the Treaty of Versailles (1919) imposed a harsh peace on Germany. The U.S. Senate never ratified the treaty.

XX

WRITTEN FOR THE SUNDAY ADVERTISER AND AMERICAN

SEPTEMBER 1, 1918

"The individual shall be protected against whatsoever force may be brought against him."

Calvin Coolidge believed in the power of free markets, but he did not make an idol of the market. This statement, written for a prominent Boston newspaper, provides more evidence that Coolidge did not serve as a tool of business as critics allege. Here he condemns "profiteering landlords" for charging high rents in wartime.

The man who seeks to stimulate and increase the production of materials necessary for the conduct of the war by raising the price he pays is a patriot. The man who refuses to sell at a fine price whatever he may have that is necessary for the conduct of the war is a profiteer. One man seeks to help his country at his own expense, the other seeks to help himself at his country's expense. One is willing to suffer himself that his country may prosper, the other is willing his country should suffer that he may prosper.

In ordinary times these difficulties are taken care of by the operation of the law of supply and demand. If the price is too high the buyer has time to go elsewhere. In war the element of time is one of the chief considerations. When what is wanted is once found it must be made available at once. The principle of trusteeship also comes into more immediate operation. It is recognized in time of peace that the public may take what it may need of private property for the general welfare, paying a fair compensation, and that the right to own property carries with it the duty of using it for the welfare of our fellow man. The time has gone by when one may do what he will with his own. He must use his property for the general good or the very right to hold private property is lost.

These are some of the rules to be observed in the relationship between man and man. To see that these rules are properly enforced, governments are formed. When they are not observed — when the strong refuse voluntary justice to the weak — then it is time for the strong arm of the law through the public officers to intervene and see that the weak are protected. This can usually be done by the enactment of a law which all will try to obey, but when this course has failed there is no remedy save by the process of law to take from the wrong-doer his power in the future to do harm.

America is built on faith in the individual, faith in his will and power to do right of his own accord, but equally is the determination that the individual shall be protected against whatsoever force may be brought against him. We believe in him not because of what he has, but what he is. But this is a practical faith. It does not rest on any silly assumption that virtue is the reward of anything but effort or that liberty can be secured at the price of anything but eternal vigilance.*

It is in recognition of these principles and conditions that the General Court of last year gave the Governor power to make rules for the use by individuals of their property during the war for the general defence of the Commonwealth, and on failure on their part so to use their property, to take possession of it for such term as may be necessary. Up to the present time it has not been necessary to take property. Our faith in the patriotism of our citizens has been amply demonstrated. Of our four millions of people few have failed voluntarily to use their every resource for the defence of the Nation. But of late there have been some complaints of too

---

* "Eternal vigilance is the price of liberty" is a famous quotation often — but wrongly — attributed to Thomas Jefferson. Researchers at Monticello have traced the statement back to the Irish statesman John Philpot Curran, who in 1790 said, "The condition upon which God hath given liberty to man is eternal vigilance."

high charges for rent in war-material centres. In some cases patriotic workmen engaged in labor most vital to our country's salvation have been threatened with eviction by profiteering landlords unless they paid exorbitant rents. No one is undertaking to say that rents must on no account be raised. But the Executive Department of Massachusetts is undertaking to say that in any case where rents are unreasonably raised to the detriment of people who are just as essential to our victory as the soldier in the field, if any one is to be evicted from such premises it will be the persons who are raising rents and not the persons who are asked to pay them. This action is taken to protect the Nation. It is taken in our desire and determination here to coöperate with the Federal Government in every activity that is necessary to the prosecution of the war. It is taken also for the protection of the individual. We do not care how humble he may be, we do not care how exalted the landlord may be, justice shall be done.

This is not to be taken as an offer on the part of the Commonwealth to have unloaded on it a large amount of property at a high price. Possession may be taken, but the ownership will not change. Unless reasonable rents are charged, the tenant will stay in possession, but the rent which the Commonwealth shall pay for occupation will be determined by a jury. This means justice, nothing more, nothing less — justice to the tenant, justice to the landlord. It is not to be inferred that our real estate owners have lacked anything as a class in patriotism. They are our most loyal, most self-sacrificing, most commendable citizens. Massachusetts by its Homestead Commission* is encouraging its citizens to own real estate because such ownership is a sheet anchor to self-government. But it is a proclamation of warning to profiteers, of approbation and approval to patriots, and of assurance and assistance to the working people and rent payers of our Commonwealth.

---

* Massachusetts created the Homestead Commission to investigate how to improve housing for the working class in crowded cities. In 1915, Massachusetts amended its constitution to allow the commission to receive state funding and actually buy land and sell homes to private citizens.

XXI

ESSEX COUNTY CLUB, LYNNFIELD

SEPTEMBER 14, 1918

"We see now that when the individual fails, whether it be from a despotism or the dead level of a socialistic state, all has failed."

Coolidge delivered this speech less than two months before the Great War ended. Here he condemns the "German military despotism" as a "conspiracy against mankind." Less than a year removed from the Bolshevik Revolution, he warns against statist and totalitarian ideologies, presciently declaring that they "are doomed to failure."

We meet here to-day as the inheritors of those principles which preserved our Nation and extended its constitutional guaranties to all its citizens. We come not as partisans but as patriots. We come to pledge anew our faith in all that America means and to declare our firm determination to defend her within and without from every foe. Above that we come to pay our tribute of wonder and admiration at the great achievements of our Nation and at the glory which they are shedding around her.

The past four years has shown the world the existence of a conspiracy against mankind of a vastness and a wickedness that could only be believed when seen in operation and confessed by its participants. This conspiracy was promoted by the German military despotism. It probably was encouraged by the results of three wars — one against Denmark which robbed her of territory, one against Austria which robbed her of territory, and one against France which robbed her of territory and a cash indemnity of a billion dollars.* These seemingly easy successes encouraged their perpetrators to plan for the pillage and enslavement of the earth.

To accomplish this, the German despotism began at home. By a systematic training the whole German people were perverted. A false idea of their own greatness was added to their contempt and hate of other nations, who, they were taught, were bent on their destruction.

---

* Under Wilhelm I and Otto von Bismarck, Prussia embarked on a series of military conquests beginning in 1864. That year, Prussia and Austria claimed a third of Denmark's territory in the German-Danish War. Less than two years later, Prussia and Austria went to war. Prussia won that conflict, the Seven Weeks' War (1866), and took over the two duchies Denmark had lost in 1864. In 1871, the Prussia-led German states defeated France. Per the harsh terms of the peace treaty, the French gave the newly created German Empire all of Alsace, half of Lorraine, and some five billion francs.

The military class were exalted and all else degraded. Thus was laid the foundation for the atrocities which have marked their conduct of the war.*

The vastness of the conquest planned has recently been revealed by August Thyssen, one of the greatest steel men of the empire.† He tells of a calling together, in the years before the war, of the industrial and banking interests of the Nation, when a plan of war was laid before them, and their support secured by the promise of spoils. France, India, Canada, Australia were to be given over to German satraps. His share was 30,000 acres in Australia, with $750,000 provided by the Government for its development. This was the promise made by the Kaiser. Here was the motive of the war.

How it was provoked is told by Prince Lichnowski, the Ambassador of Germany to London.‡ He shows how he had reached agreements for a treaty which would show the good will of Great Britain. Berlin refused to sign it unless it should be kept secret. He shows how

---

* During the Great War, Germany committed atrocities against Belgian and French civilians, used chemical weapons, and conducted unrestricted submarine warfare.

† German industrialist August Thyssen (1842–1926) made his fortune producing millions of tons of steel and iron. He became known as the "Rockefeller of the Ruhr."

‡ Prince Karl Max von Lichnowsky (Coolidge uses a different spelling) served as Germany's ambassador to the United Kingdom in the leadup to war. Coolidge refers to a pamphlet Lichnowsky wrote and privately circulated in 1916, in which the former ambassador condemned German diplomacy for provoking war. The pamphlet later went public.

Germany used Austria to attack Serbia; how mediations were refused; when Austria was about to withdraw, Germany sent an ultimatum to Russia one day and the next day declared war.

This diplomat sums up the whole case when he says: "I had to support in London a policy the heresy of which I recognized. That brought down vengeance on me because it was a sin against the Holy Ghost." What an indictment of Germany from her own confession! A plan to use the revelations of science for the sack and slavery of the earth; the degradation, perversion, corruption of a whole people, and by those who should have been the wardens of their righteousness, done for the temporal glory of a military caste, and all in the name of divine right.

Much of this was not known in America when we declared war. It is with great difficulty we realize it now. We had seen Germany going from infamy to infamy. We did know of the violated treaty of Belgium, of the piracy, the murder of women and children, the destruction of the property and lives of our neutral citizens, and finally the plain declaration of the German Imperial Government that it would wantonly and purposely destroy the property and lives of any American citizen who exercised his undoubted legal right to sail certain portions of the sea. This attempt to declare law for America by an edict from Potsdam we resisted by the sword. We see at last not only the hideous wickedness which perpetrated the war, we see that it is a world war, that Germany struck not only at Belgium, she struck at us, she struck at our whole system of civilization. A wicked purpose, which a vain attempt to realize has involved its authors in more and more wickedness. We hear that even among the civil population of Germany crime is rampant.

Looking now at this condition of Germany and her Allies, it is time to inquire what America and her Allies have to offer as a remedy, and what effect the application of such remedy has had upon ourselves. We have drawn the sword, but is it only to

"Be blood for blood, for treason treachery"?*

Are we seeking merely to match infamy with infamy, merely to pillage and destroy those who threatened to pillage and destroy us? No; we have taken more than the sword, lest we perish by the sword; we have summoned the moral power of the Nation. We have recognized that evil is only to be overcome by good. We have marshalled the righteousness of America to overwhelm the wickedness of Germany. A new spirit has come over the nation the like of which was never seen before. We can see it not only in the new purity of camp life, in the heroism of our soldiers as they fight in the faith and

---

* From Sir Walter Scott's poem "The Vision of Don Roderick" (1811), which celebrated the Duke of Wellington's victories in the Peninsular Campaign.

for the faith of the fathers, but we see it in the healing influences which a righteous purpose has had upon the evils which beset us.

We entered the war a people of many nationalities. We are united now; every one is first an American. We were beset with jealousies, and envy, and class prejudice. Service in the camp has taught each soldier to respect the other, whatever his source, and a mutual sympathy at home has brought all into a common citizenship. The service flag is a great leveller.

Our industrial life has been purified of prejudice. No one is complaining now that any concern is too large, too strong. All see that the great organizations of capital in industry are our salvation. Labor has taken on a new dignity and nobility. When the idle see the necessity of work, when we begin to recognize industry as essential, the working man begins to have paid him the honor which is his due.

Invention, chemistry, medicine, surgery, have been stimulated and improved. Even our agriculture has taken on more economical methods and increased production.

The call for man power has given a new idea of the importance of the individual, so that there has been brought to the humblest the knowledge that he was not only important but his importance was realized. And with this has come the discovery of new powers, not only in the slouch whom military drill has transformed into a man, but to labor that has found a new joy, satisfaction and efficiency in its work. The entire activities of the Nation are tuned up.

The spirit of charity has been aroused. Hundreds of millions have been provided by voluntary gifts for the Red Cross, Knights of Columbus, Hebrew Charities, and Christian Associations. The people are turning to their places of worship with a new religious fervor. Everywhere selfishness is giving way to service, idleness to industry, wastefulness to thrift.

The war is being won. It is being overwhelmingly won. A righteous purpose has not only strengthened our arms abroad but exalted the Nation at home.

The great work before us is to keep this new spirit in the right path. The opportunity for a military training, the beneficial results of its discipline, must be continued for the youth of our country. The sacrifice necessary for national defence must hereafter never be neglected. The virtues of war must be carried into peace.* But this must not be done at the expense of the freedom of the individual. It must be the expression of self-government and not the despotism of a German military caste or a Russian Bolshevik state. We are in this war to preserve

---

* When the United States declared war on Germany in April 1917, its standing army included only 127,500 men. More than four million served in the U.S. armed forces during the war. The military ended the draft at war's end, but the National Defense Act of 1920 expanded the maximum peacetime strength of both the U.S. Army and the National Guard.

the institutions that have made us great. The war has revealed to us their true greatness. All argument about the efficiency of despotism and the incompetence of republics was answered at the Marne* and will be hereafter answered at the Rhine.† We are not going to overcome the Kaiser by becoming like him, nor aid Russia by becoming like her.

We see now that Prussian despotism was the natural ally of the Russian Bolshevik and the I.W.W. here.‡ Both exist to pervert and enslave the people; both seek to break down the national spirit of the world for their own wicked ends. Both are doomed to failure. By taking our place in the world, America is to become more American, as by doing his duty the individual develops his own manhood. We see now that when the individual fails, whether it be from a despotism or the dead level of a socialistic state, all has failed.

A new vision has come to the Nation, a vision that must never be obscured. It is for us to heed it, to follow it. It is a revelation, but a revelation not of our weakness

---

* Two months before this speech, at the Second Battle of the Marne, Allied forces in France repelled the last major German offensive of the war. At the First Battle of the Marne, in September 1914, the Allies had thrown back another German assault, saving Paris.

† Five weeks before Coolidge spoke, the Allies had begun the Hundred Days Offensive, which would end the war in November.

‡ The IWW refers to the International Workers of the World, a radical labor union nicknamed the Wobblies. Socialists and anarchists figured prominently in the organization.

but of our strength, not of new principles, but of the power that lies in the application of old doctrines. May that vision never fade, may America inspired by a great purpose ever be able to say,

"Mine eyes have seen the glory of the coming of the Lord."

XXII

TREMONT TEMPLE

NOVEMBER 2, 1918

"There is no greater service that we can render
the oppressed of the earth than to maintain
inviolate the freedom of our own citizens."

*Coolidge gave this address in Boston three days before Elec-
tion Day and nine days before the armistice. For a state
politician, the entire experience of mobilization, sending
troops overseas, and now their return and the attendant
diplomacy represented a kind of bath in foreign policy that
would serve Coolidge later as vice president and president.
Here he recognizes the bravery, honor, and integrity of the
soldiers fighting in Europe, as well as the righteousness of
their cause. He also looks ahead to the responsibilities that
will come when the war ends.*

To the greatest task man ever undertook our Commonwealth has applied itself, will continue to apply itself

with no laggard hand. One hundred and ninety thousand
of her sons already in the field, hundreds of millions of
her treasure contributed to the cause, her entire citizenship moved with a single purpose, all these show a determination unalterable, to prosecute the war to a victory so
conclusive, to a destruction of all enemy forces so decisive,
that those impious pretentions which have threatened the
earth for many years will never be renewed. There can be
no discussion about it, there can be no negotiation about
it. The country is united in the conviction that the only
terms are unconditional surrender.

This determination has arisen from no sudden
impulse or selfish motive. It was forced upon us by the
plan and policy of Germany and her methods of waging
war upon others. The main features of it all have long
been revealed while each day brings to light more of
the details. We have seen the studied effort to make
perverts of sixty millions of German people. We know
of the corrupting of the business interests of the Empire
to secure their support. We know that war had been
decreed before the pretext on which it was declared had
happened. We know Austria was and is the creature of
Germany. We have beheld the violation of innocent Belgium, the hideous outrages on soldier and civilian, the
piracy, the murder of our own neutral citizens, and finally
there came the notice, which as an insult to America has
been exceeded only by the recent suggestion that we
negotiate a peace with its authors, — the notice claiming

dominion over our citizens and authority to exclude our ships from the sea. The great pretender to the throne of the earth thought the time had come to assert that we were his subjects. Two millions of our men already in France, and each day ten thousand more are hastening to pay their respects to him at his court in Berlin in person. He has our answer.

It would be a mistake to suppose we have already won the war. It is not won yet, but we have reached the place where we know how to win it, and if we continue our exertions we shall win it fully, completely, grandly, as becomes a great people contending for the cause of righteousness.

We entered the war late and without previous military preparation. The more clearly we discern the beginning and the progress of the struggle, the more we must admire the great spirit of those nations by whose side we fight. The more we know of the terrible price they paid, the matchless sacrifices they magnificently endured — the French, the Italians, the British, the Belgians, the Serbians, the Poles, and the misgoverned, misguided people of Russia — the bravery of their soldiers in the field, the unflinching devotion of their people at home, and remember that in no small sense they were doing this for us, that we have been the direct beneficiaries of peoples who have given their all, the less disposition we have to think too much of our own importance. But all this should not cause us to withhold the praise that is due our own Army and Navy, or to overlook the fact that our people have met every call that patriotism has made. The soldiers and sailors who fight under the Stars and Stripes are the most magnificent body of men that ever took up arms for defence of a great cause. Man for man they surpass any other troops on earth.

We must not forget these things. We must not neglect to record them for the information of generations to come. The names and records of boards and commissions, relief societies, of all who have engaged in financing the cause of government and charity, and other patriotic work, should be preserved in the Library of the Commonwealth, and with these, our military achievements. These will show how American soldiers met and defeated the Prussian Guard. They will show also that in all the war no single accomplishment, on a like scale, excelled the battle of St. Mihiel,* carried out by American troops, with our own Massachusetts boys among them, and that the first regiment to be decorated as a regiment for conspicuous service and gallantry in our Army in France was the 104th, formerly of the old Massachusetts National Guard.† Such is our record and it cannot be forgotten.

---

* The Battle of Saint-Mihiel, in northeastern France, took place in September 1918. It represented the first offensive in the Great War that U.S. forces led. A young George Patton commanded the tank assault from the front lines.

† French military leaders awarded the 104th Infantry Regiment the Croix de Guerre. The 104th thus became the first American unit to receive a military decoration from a foreign country.

In reaching the great decision to enter the war, in preparing the answer which speaks with so much authority, in the only language that despotism can understand, America has arisen to a new life. We have taken a new place among the nations. The Revolution made us a nation; the Spanish War made us a world power,* the present war has given us recognition as a world power. We shall not again be considered provincial. Whether we desired it or not this position has come to us with its duties and its responsibilities.

This new position should not be misunderstood. It does not mean any diminution of our national spirit. It rather means that it should be intensified. The most outstanding feature of the war has been the assertion of the national spirit. Each nationality is contending for the right to have its own government, and in that is meeting with the sanction of the free peoples of the earth. We are discussing a league of nations. Such a league, if formed, is not for the purpose, must not be for the purpose, of diminishing the spirit or influence of our Nation, but to make that spirit and influence more real and more effective.† Believing in our Nation thoroughly

---

* After its victory in the Spanish-American War (1898), the United States gained control of the Philippines, Puerto Rico, and Guam. Spain also relinquished its claim to Cuba.

† Coolidge remained ambivalent about the League of Nations. In February 1919, as governor, he warmly welcomed President Woodrow Wilson to Massachusetts when Wilson arrived to promote the League of Nations. Yet Coolidge refused to tell reporters his opinion of the league. In 1923, after the U.S. Senate

and unreservedly, confident that the evidence of the past and present justifies that belief, it is our one desire to make America more American. There is no greater service that we can render the oppressed of the earth than to maintain inviolate the freedom of our own citizens.

Under our National Government the States are the sheet-anchors of our institutions. On them falls the task of administering local affairs and of supporting the National Government in peace and war. The success with which Massachusetts has met her local problems, the efficiency with which she has placed her resources of men and materials at the disposal of the Nation, has been unsurpassed. The efficient organization of the Commonwealth, which has proved itself in time of stress, must be maintained undiminished. On the States will largely fall the task of putting into effect the lessons of the war that are to make America more truly American.

One of our first duties is military training. The opportunity hereafter for the youth of the Nation to receive instruction in the science of national defence should be universal. The great problem which our present experience has brought is the development of man power. This includes many questions, but especially public health and mental equipment. Sanitation and education will require more attention in the future.

---

rejected the League of Nations treaty, President Coolidge said, "The United States sees no reason to limit its own freedom and independence of action by joining [the league]."

America has been performing a great service for humanity. In that service we have arisen to a new glory. The people of the nation without distinction have been performing a great service for America. In it they have realized a new citizenship. Prussianism fails. Americanism succeeds. Education is to teach men not what to think but how to think. Government will take on new activities, but it is not more to control the people, the people are more to control the Government.

We have come to the realization of a new brotherhood among nations and among men. It came through the performance of a common duty. A brotherhood that existed unseen has been recognized at last by those called to the camp and trenches and those working for their victory at home. This spirit must not be misunderstood. It is not a gospel of ease but of work, not of dependence but of independence, not of an easy tolerance of wrong but a stern insistence on right, not the privilege of receiving but the duty of giving.

"Man proposes but God disposes."* When Germany lit up her long toasted day with the lurid glare of war, she thought the end of freedom for the peoples of the earth had come. She thought that the power of her sword was hereafter to reign supreme over a world in slavery, and that the divine right of a king was to be established

---

* The phrase comes from *The Imitation of Christ*, Thomas à Kempis's fifteenth-century classic. In the original Latin, the phrase reads, "Homo proponit, sed Deus disponit."

forever. We have seen the drama drawing to its close. It has shown the victory of justice and of freedom and established the divine rights of the people. Through it is shining a new revelation of the true brotherhood of man. As we see the purpose Germany sought and the result she will secure, the words of Holy Writ come back to us — "The wrath of man shall praise Him."*

---

* Psalm 76:10: "Surely the wrath of man shall praise thee: the remainder of wrath shalt thou restrain."

XXIII

FANEUIL HALL

"To save America means to save
American institutions."

*During the 1918 gubernatorial campaign, Coolidge largely
avoided discussing state issues, confident that he held the
advantage against his Democratic opponent, Richard Long.
That remained true even on the eve of Election Day. In
this speech, Coolidge again focuses on the Great War and
America's future. He does, however, begin by alluding to the
Democrats' attacks on him.*

We need a word of caution and of warning. I am
responsible for what I have said and what I have
done. I am not responsible for what my opponents say
I have said or say I have done either on the stump or
in untrue political advertisements and untrue posters. I

shall not deal with these. I do not care to touch them, but I do not want any of my fellow citizens to misunderstand my ignoring them as expressing any attitude other than considering such attempts unworthy of notice when men are fighting for the preservation of our country.*

Our work is drawing to a close — our patriotic efforts. We have had in view but one object — the saving of America.

We shall accomplish that object first by winning the war. That means a great deal. It means getting the world forever rid of the German idea. We can see no way to do this but by a complete surrender by Germany to the Allies.

We stand by the State and National Governments in the prosecution of this object. I have reiterated that we support the Commander-in-Chief in war work. He says that is so.

We want no delay in prosecuting the war. The quickest way is the way to save most lives and treasure. We want to care for the soldiers and their dependents. That has been the recognized duty of the Government for generations.

To save America means to save American institutions, it means to save the manhood and womanhood of our country. To that we are pledged.

---

* Richard Long's supporters ran advertisements claiming that Coolidge had no real accomplishments and had not fully supported President Wilson's war programs. Coolidge's biggest backer, Frank Stearns, angrily prepared an ad to counter the attacks. Coolidge refused to run it.

There will be great questions of reconstruction, social, industrial, economic and governmental questions, that must be met and solved. They must be met with a recognition of a new spirit.

It is a time to keep our faith in our State, our Nation, our institutions, and in each other. Doing that, the war will be won in the field and won in civil life at home.

XXIV

FROM INAUGURAL ADDRESS
AS GOVERNOR

JANUARY 2, 1919

"Can we still act on the principle that there is
no sacrifice too great to maintain the right?"

*Coolidge prevailed in the 1918 governor's race. At his inaugu-
ration in the new year, he called on legislators' sense of duty,
much as he had in his 1914 "Have Faith in Massachusetts"
address. This speech sounds familiar Coolidge themes,
including responsibility, duty, loyalty, industry, and thrift.
Readers may note the length of the speech — short. Coolidge
had begun to make a practice of short speeches in the hope
his own concision would inspire. He once counseled: "And be
brief. Above all things, be brief."*

You are coming to a new legislative session under
the inspiration of the greatest achievements in all
history. You are beholding the fulfilment of the age-old

promise, man coming into his own. You are to have
the opportunity and responsibility of reflecting this new
spirit in the laws of the most enlightened of Common-
wealths. We must steadily advance. Each individual
must have the rewards and opportunities worthy of the
character of our citizenship, a broader recognition of
his worth and a larger liberty, protected by order —
and always under the law. In the promotion of human
welfare Massachusetts happily may not need much
reconstruction, but, like all living organizations, forever
needs continuing construction.* What are the lessons of
the past? How shall they be applied to these days of
readjustment? How shall we emerge from the autocratic
methods of war to the democratic methods of peace,
raising ourselves again to the source of all our strength
and all our glory — sound self-government?

It is your duty not only to reflect public opinion, but
to lead it. Whether we are to enter a new era in Massachusetts depends upon you. The lessons of the war are
plain. Can we carry them on into peace? Can we still
act on the principle that there is no sacrifice too great
to maintain the right? Shall we continue to advocate and

---

* Like the rest of the country, Massachusetts needed to adjust to postwar
realities, including reintegrating masses of servicemen into civilian life and
reestablishing a peacetime economy. Massachusetts had also approved a plan
to consolidate state government. As a result, the new governor needed to pare
more than a hundred departments down to twenty — and to lay off state
employees in the process.

practise thrift and industry? Shall we require unswerving loyalty to our country? These are the foundations of all greatness.

Let there be a purpose in all your legislation to recognize the right of man to be well born, well nurtured, well educated, well employed, and well paid. This is no gospel of ease and selfishness, or class distinction, but a gospel of effort and service, of universal application.

Such results cannot be secured at once, but they should be ever before us. The world has assumed burdens that will bear heavily on all peoples. We shall not escape our share. But whatever may be our trials, however difficult our tasks, they are only the problems of peace, and a victorious peace. The war is over. Whatever the call of duty now we should remember with gratitude that it is nothing compared with the heavy sacrifice so lately made. The genius and fortitude which conquered then cannot now fail.

XXV

STATEMENT ON THE DEATH
OF THEODORE ROOSEVELT

"During the almost eight years [Roosevelt] was
President, the people came to see in him a reflection
of their ideals of the true Americanism."

Theodore Roosevelt died on January 6, 1919. Sending this
eulogy thus became one of Coolidge's first acts as governor.
Roosevelt and Coolidge appeared as opposites: Roosevelt the
exuberant personality and active executive versus Silent Cal,
who believed in executive restraint. Yet Coolidge admired
Roosevelt and, especially early in his career, aligned with the
president on many progressive policies.

The people of our Commonwealth have learned
with profound sorrow of the death of Theodore
Roosevelt. No other citizen of the Nation would have
brought in so large a degree the feeling of a common
loss. During the almost eight years he was President, the

people came to see in him a reflection of their ideals of the true Americanism.

He was the advocate of every good cause. He awakened the moral purpose of the Nation and raised the standard of public service. He appealed to the imagination of youth and satisfied the judgment of maturity. In him Massachusetts saw an exponent of her own ideals.

In token of the love and reverence which all the people bore him, I urge that the national and state flags be flown at half-mast throughout the Commonwealth until after his funeral, and that, when next the people gather for public worship, his loss be marked with proper ceremony.

XXVI

LINCOLN DAY PROCLAMATION

JANUARY 30, 1919

"Men show by what they worship what they are."

As a Republican, Coolidge naturally cited the party's most popular hero, President Lincoln. But Coolidge's interest in Honest Abe went beyond the political. Soon after issuing this proclamation, Coolidge penned an introduction to Carl Schurz's short biography of Lincoln. In that introduction, Coolidge praised the humility of Lincoln and pressed back against the habit of deifying him: "To idealize him destroys him. The greatest inspiration his life can give is in the whole truth about him. Leave him as he is." Here, Coolidge focuses on the story of Lincoln's mother, who, like his own, passed away while her son was a boy. Coolidge also notes Lincoln's ability to deal with practical affairs — to find the middle ground, and to sacrifice his own popularity to the cause.

The Commonwealth of Massachusetts
By His Excellency Calvin Coolidge, Governor

A PROCLAMATION

F ivescore and ten years ago that Divine Providence
which infinite repetition has made only the more a
miracle sent into the world a new life, destined to save
a nation. No star, no sign, foretold his coming. About
his cradle all was poor and mean save only the source
of all great men, the love of a wonderful woman. When
she faded way in his tender years, from her deathbed in
humble poverty she dowered her son with greatness.*
There can be no proper observance of a birthday which
forgets the mother. Into his origin as into his life men
long have looked and wondered. In wisdom great, but
in humility greater, in justice strong, but in compassion
stronger, he became a leader of men by being a follower
of the truth. He overcame evil with good. His presence
filled the Nation. He broke the might of oppression.
He restored a race to its birthright. His mortal frame
has vanished, but his spirit increases with the increasing
years, the richest legacy of the greatest century.

Men show by what they worship what they are. It is

---

* Like Coolidge, Lincoln lost his mother when he was a boy. Coolidge was
twelve when his mother died; Lincoln was nine. Coolidge supporters included
these comments about Nancy Lincoln in a special booklet of quotations they
prepared for delegates at the 1920 Republican National Convention.

no accident that before the great example of American manhood our people stand with respect and reverence. And in accordance with this sentiment our laws have provided for a formal recognition of the birthday of Abraham Lincoln, for in him is revealed our ideal, the hope of our country fulfilled.

Now, therefore, by the authority of Massachusetts, the 12th day of February is set apart as

LINCOLN DAY

and its observance recommended as befits the beneficiaries of his life and the admirers of his character, in places of education and worship wherever our people meet one with another.

Given at the Executive Chamber, in Boston, this 30th day of January, in the year of Our Lord one thousand nine hundred and nineteen, and of the independence of the United States of America the one hundred and forty-third.

By His Excellency the Governor,   CALVIN COOLIDGE

ALBERT P. LANGTRY,
Secretary of the Commonwealth.

God save the Commonwealth of Massachusetts.

XXVII

INTRODUCING HENRY CABOT LODGE AND A. LAWRENCE LOWELL AT THE DEBATE ON THE LEAGUE OF NATIONS, SYMPHONY HALL

March 19, 1919

"All America has but one desire, the security
of the peace by facts and by parchment which
her brave sons have wrought by the sword."

*In 1919, the question of whether the United States should
enter the League of Nations became contentious. Henry
Cabot Lodge, who represented Massachusetts in the Senate
for more than thirty years, led the GOP opposition to the
league. At Boston's Symphony Hall, Lodge debated Harvard
University president A. Lawrence Lowell, a prominent supporter of the League of Nations. Governor Coolidge, who
displayed ambivalence toward the league, introduced the
debaters.*

We meet here as representatives of a great people
to listen to the discussion of a great question by
great men. All America has but one desire, the security

of the peace by facts and by parchment which her brave sons have wrought by the sword. It is a duty we owe alike to the living and the dead.

Fortunate is Massachusetts that she has among her sons two men so eminently trained for the task of our enlightenment, a senior Senator of the Commonwealth and the President of a university established in her Constitution. Wherever statesmen gather, wherever men love letters, this day's discussion will be read and pondered. Of these great men in learning, and experience, wise in the science and practice of government, the first to address you is a Senator distinguished at home and famous everywhere — Henry Cabot Lodge.

[After Senator Lodge spoke he introduced President Lowell:]

The next to address you is the President of Harvard University — an educator renowned throughout the world, a learned student of statesmanship, endowed with a wisdom which has made him a leader of men, truly a Master of Arts, eminently a Doctor of Laws, a fitting representative of the Massachusetts domain of letters — Abbott Lawrence Lowell.

XXVIII

VETO OF SALARY INCREASE

*"The realities of life are not measured
by dollars and cents."*

*In 1919, Governor Coolidge exercised his veto power when
members of the Massachusetts legislature awarded themselves
a 50 percent pay raise. His remarks here reflect his belief that
public service represents an "avocation" (see page 73). The legislature overrode his veto, but the* Boston Herald *said it had
never seen a "clearer or more admirable veto message."*

To the Honorable Senate and House of Representatives:

In accordance with the duty imposed by the Constitution, a bill entitled, "An act to establish the compensation of the members of the General Court," being
House No. 1629, is herewith returned without approval.

This bill raises the salaries of members from $1000 to $1500, an increase of fifty per cent, and is retroactive. It is necessary to decide whether the Commonwealth can well afford this additional tax and whether any public benefit would accrue from it.

These are times that require careful scrutiny of public expenditure. The burden of taxes resulting from war is heavy. The addition of $142,000 to the expense of the Commonwealth in perpetuity is not to be undertaken but upon proven necessity.

Service in the General Court is not obligatory but optional. It is not to be undertaken as a profession or a means of livelihood. It is a voluntary public service. In accord with the principles of our democratic institutions a compensation has been given in order that talent for service rather than the possession of property might be the standard of membership. There is no man of sufficient talent in the Commonwealth so poor that he cannot serve for a session, which averages about five months, and five days each week, at a salary of $1000 — and travel allowance of $2.50 for each mile between his home and the State House. This is too clear for argument. There is no need to consider those who are too rich to serve for this sum. It would be futile to discuss whether their services are worth more or less than this, as that is not here the question. Membership in the General Court is not a job. There are services rendered to the Commonwealth by senators and representatives that are priceless. For the searching out of great principles on which legislation is based there is no adequate compensation. If value for services were the criterion, there would be 280 different salaries. When membership is sought as a means of livelihood, legislation will pass from a public function to a private enterprise. Men do not serve here for pay. They seek work and places of responsibility and find in that seeking, not in their pay, their honor.

The realities of life are not measured by dollars and cents. The skill of the physician, the divine eloquence of the clergyman, the courage of the soldier, that which we call character in all men, are not matters of hire and salary. No person was ever honored for what he received. Honor has been the reward for what he gave. Public acclaim and the ceremonious recognition paid to returning heroes are not on account of their government pay but of the service and sacrifice they gave their country. The place each member of the General Court will hold in the estimation of his constituents will never depend on his salary, but on the ability and integrity with which he does his duty; not on what he receives, but on what he gives; and only out of the bountifulness of his own giving will his constituents raise him to power. Not by indulging himself, but by denying himself, will he reach success.

It is because the General Court has recognized these principles in its past history that it has secured its high place as a legislative body. This act disregards all this and will ever appear to be an undertaking by members to raise their own salaries. The fact that many were thinking of the needs of others will remain unknown. Appearances cannot be disregarded. Those in whom is placed the solemn duty of caring for others ought to think of themselves last or their decisions will lack authority. There is apparent a disposition to deny the disinterestedness and impartiality of government. Such charges are the result of ignorance and an evil desire to destroy our institutions for personal profit. It is of infinite importance to demonstrate that legislation is used not for the benefit of the legislator, but of the public.

The General Court of Massachusetts is a legislative body noted for its fairness and ability. It has no superior. Its critics have for the most part come from the outside and have most frequently been those who have approached it with the purpose of securing selfish desires of their clients or themselves. A long familiarity with it increases respect for it. It is charged with expressing the abiding convictions and conscience of the people of the Commonwealth. The most solemn obligation placed by the Constitution on the Executive is the power to veto its actions. In all matters affecting it the General Court is entitled to his best judgment and carefully considered opinion. Anything less would be a mark of disrespect and disloyalty to its members. That judgment and opinion, arrived at after a wide counsel with members and others, is here expressed, in the light of an obligation which is not personal, "faithfully and impartially to discharge and perform" the duties of a public office.

XXIX

FLAG DAY PROCLAMATION

MAY 26, 1919

"What could be saved if the flag of the
American Nation were to perish?"

In this proclamation recognizing June 14 as Flag Day, Governor Coolidge extols the great principle for which the American flag stands: "the sovereignty of the people."

W orks which endure come from the soul of the people. The mighty in their pride walk alone to destruction. The humble walk hand in hand with Providence to immortality. Their works survive. When the people of the Colonies were defending their liberties against the might of kings, they chose their banner from the design set in the firmament through all eternity. The flags of the great empires of that day are gone, but the Stars and Stripes remain. It pictures the vision of a people whose eyes were turned to the rising dawn. It represents the hope of a father for his posterity. It was never flaunted for the glory of royalty, but to be born under it is to be a child of a king, and to establish a home under it is to be the founder of a royal house. Alone of all flags it expresses the sovereignty of the people which endures when all else passes away. Speaking with their voice it has the sanctity of revelation. He who lives under it and is loyal to it is loyal to truth and justice everywhere. He who lives under it and is disloyal to it is a traitor to the human race everywhere. What could be saved if the flag of the American Nation were to perish?

In recognition of these truths and out of a desire born of a purpose to defend and perpetuate them, the Commonwealth of Massachusetts has by ordinance decreed that for one day of each year their importance should be dwelt upon and remembered. Therefore, in accordance with that authority, the anniversary of the adoption of the national flag, the 14th day of June next, is set apart as

FLAG DAY

and it is earnestly recommended that it be observed by the people of the Commonwealth by the display of the flag of our country and in all ways that may testify to their loyalty and perpetuate its glory.

XXX

AMHERST COLLEGE
COMMENCEMENT

JUNE 18, 1919

"If society lacks learning and virtue, it perishes."

Twenty-four years after graduating from Amherst, Coolidge gave the commencement address at his alma mater. Far more than a tribute to Amherst, this address makes a powerful case for a liberal education ("A vocational or technical education is not enough"). Coolidge also offers a defense of the Western tradition.

To the son of any college, although he does not make his connection with his college a profession, a return of Commencement Day recalls many memories. It is likely also, after nearly a quarter of a century, to cause some reflections. It is, I suppose, to give tongue to such memories and reflections that after-dinner speaking is provided.

After all due allowance for change of perspective, going to college was a greater event twenty-five years ago than it is to-day. My own memories are not yet ancient enough to warrant their recalling. The greater events of that day are too recent to need to be related.

But I should fail in my duty and neglect my deep conviction if I did not declare that in my day there was no better place to educate a young man. Most of them came with a realization that their coming meant a sacrifice at home. They may have lacked a proficiency in the arts of the drawing room which sometimes brought a smile; but no competitor met the Amherst men of that day on the athletic field or in the postgraduate school with a smile that did not soon come off. They had their pranks and sprees, but they had the ideals of a true manhood. They were moved with a serious purpose. He who had less lacked place among them. They are come and gone from the campus, those men of the early nineties, and with them went the power to command.

Those were days that represented especially the spirit of President Seelye.* Under his brilliant and polished successor the Faculty changes were few. There was Professor Wood,† the most accomplished intellectual hazer

---

* Julius H. Seelye served as president of Amherst College from 1876 to 1890. He had previously served in the U.S. House of Representatives. Merrill E. Gates succeeded Seelye as Amherst president.

† E. Lincoln Wood, professor of Latin.

of freshmen. There was Professor Gibbons,* who was strong enough in Greek derivation so that every second-year man soon had a clear conception of the meaning of sophomore. After demonstrating clearly that on the negative side the derivation of "contiguity" was not "con" and "tiguity," he advised those who could not with equal clearness demonstrate its derivation on the positive side to look it up. There were Morse and Frink, Richardson, Hitchcock, Estey, Crowell, Tyler, and Garman.† All these and more are gone. The living, no less eminent, I need not recall. As a teaching force, as an inspirer of youth, for training men how to think, that faculty has had and will have nowhere any superior.

"So passed that pageant."‡

The college of to-day has taken on a new life, a new activity. Military training then was a spectacle for the

---

* Henry Gibbons, professor of Greek.

† Anson D. Morse, professor of history and political economy; Henry A. Frink, professor of logic and oratory; Henry B. Richardson, professor of German; Edward Hitchcock, professor of hygiene and physical education; William C. Esty (Coolidge misspells the name), professor of mathematics and astronomy; Edward P. Crowell, professor of Latin language and literature; William Seymour Tyler, professor of Greek language and literature (whom Coolidge described as "a patriarch in appearance with a long beard and flowing white hair"); and Charles E. Garman, professor of mental philosophy — an influence on Coolidge.

‡ From Sir Walter Scott's poem "The Vision of Don Roderick" (1811). The full line reads: "So passed that pageant. Ere another came."

Massachusetts Agricultural College.* To-day Amherst welcomes its returning soldiers, and but a little time since divested itself of the character of a military camp to resume the wonted garb of peace. Yet it is and has been the same institution, — a college of the liberal arts. In this so-called practical age Amherst has chosen for her province the most practical of all, — the culture and the classics of all time.

Civilization depends not only upon the knowledge of the people, but upon the use they make of it. If knowledge be wrongfully used, civilization commits suicide. Broadly speaking, the college is not to educate the individual, but to educate society. The individual may be ignorant and vicious. If society have learning and virtue, that will sustain him. If society lacks learning and virtue, it perishes. Education must give not only power but direction. It must minister to the whole man or it fails.

Such an education considered from the position of society does not come from science. That provides power alone, but not direction. Give a savage tribe firearms and a distillery, and their members will exterminate each other. They have science all right, but misuse it. They lack ideals. These young men that we welcome back with so much pride did not go forth to demonstrate their faith in science. They did not offer their lives because of

* Massachusetts Agricultural College ultimately became the University of Massachusetts Amherst.

their belief in any rule of mathematics or any principle of physics or chemistry. The laws of the natural world would be unaffected by their defeat or victory. No; they were defending their ideals, and those ideals came from the classics.

This is preëminently true of the culture of Greece and Rome. Patriotism with them was predominant. Their heroes were those who sacrificed themselves for their country, from the three hundred at Thermopylae* to Horatius at the bridge.† Their poets sang of the glory of dying for one's native land. The orations of Demosthenes and Cicero are pitched in the same high strain. The philosophy of Plato and Aristotle and the Greek and Latin classics were the foundation of the Renaissance. The revival of learning was the revival of Athens and Sparta and of the Imperial City. Modern science is their product. To be included with the classics are modern history and literature, the philosophers, the orators, the statesmen, and poets, — Milton and Shakespeare, Lowell and Whittier,‡ — the Farewell Address, the

---

* In 480 BC, the Spartan king Leonidas led a vastly outnumbered force in a valiant attempt to hold the Thermopylae pass against the powerful Persian army. Almost every one of the three hundred Spartans fought to the death, including Leonidas.

† Thomas Babington Macaulay's famous poem "Horatius at the Bridge" (1842) recounts how, in ancient Rome, Horatius Cocles heroically faced the Etruscan army to hold the bridge that crossed the Tiber.

‡ The popular nineteenth-century poets James Russell Lowell and John Greenleaf Whittier.

Reply to Hayne,* the Speech at Gettysburg, — it is all these and more that I mean by the classics. They give not only power to the intellect, but direct its course of action.

The classic of all classics is the Bible.

I do not underestimate schools of science and technical arts. They have a high and noble calling in ministering to mankind. They are important and necessary. I am pointing out that in my opinion they do not provide a civilization that can stand without the support of the ideals that come from the classics.

The conclusion to be derived from this position is that a vocational or technical education is not enough. We must have every American citizen well grounded in the classical ideals. Such an education will not unfit him for the work of the world. Did those men in the trenches fight any less valiantly, did they shrink any more from the hardships of war, when a liberal culture had given a broader vision of what the great conflict meant? The discontent in modern industry is the result of a too narrow outlook. A more liberal culture will reveal the importance and nobility of the work of the world, whether in war or peace. It is far from enough to teach our citizens a vocation. Our industrial system will break down unless it is humanized. There is greater

* Senator Daniel Webster's famous response to Senator Robert Hayne of South Carolina during the nullification dispute in January 1830.

need for a liberal culture that will develop the whole man in the whole body of our citizenship. The day when a college education will be the portion of all may not be so far distant as it seems.

We live in a republic. Our Government is exercised through representatives. Their course of action is a very accurate reflection of public opinion. Where shall that be formed and directed unless from the influences, direct and indirect, that come from our institutions of learning? The laws of a republic represent its ideals. They are founded upon public opinion, and public opinion in America up to the present time has drawn its inspiration from the classics. They tell us that Waterloo was won on the football fields of Rugby and Eton. The German war was won by the influence of classical ideals. As a teacher of the classics, as a maker of public opinion, as a source of wise laws, as the herald of a righteous victory, — Amherst College stands on a foundation which has remained unchanged through the ages. May there be in all her sons a conviction that with her abides Him who changes not.

XXXI

HARVARD UNIVERSITY
COMMENCEMENT

JUNE 19, 1919

"In our pursuit of prosperity we have
forgotten and neglected its foundations."

The day after speaking at Amherst, Coolidge addressed Harvard's graduating class. Here he calls on Harvard alumni to serve as defenders "of righteous convictions, of reverence for truth and for the heralds of truth." Coolidge warns of the limits of materialism, saying, "We have lost our reverence for the profession of teaching and bestowed it upon the profession of acquiring."

No college man who has ever glanced at the Constitution of Massachusetts is likely to miss or forget the generous references there made to Harvard University. It may need a closer study of that instrument, which is older than the American Constitution, to realize the full significance of those most enduring of guaranties that could then be imposed in behalf of Massachusetts institutions.

The convention which framed our Constitution has as its president James Bowdoin, a son of Harvard. He was a man of great strength of character and cast an influence for good upon the deliberations of his day worthy of a place in history more conspicuous than is generally accorded to him. He had as his colleague on the floor no less a person than John Adams. It is not necessary in this presence to designate his alma mater. There were others of importance, but these represented the type of thought that prevailed.

In that noble Declaration of Rights the principles of freedom and equality were first declared. Following this is set forth the right of religious liberty and the duty of citizens to support places of religious worship and instruction; and in the Frame of Government, after establishing the University, there is given to legislators and magistrates a mandate forever to cherish and support the cause of education and institutions of learning. These were the declaration of broad and liberal policies. They are capable of being combined, for in fact they declare that teaching, whether it be by clergy or laity, is of an importance that requires it to be surrounded with the same safeguards and guaranties as freedom and equality. In fact the Constitution declares that "wisdom and knowledge, as well as virtue, diffused generally among the body of the people, are necessary for the preservation of their rights and liberties." John Adams and James Bowdoin knew that freedom was the fruit of knowledge. Their conclusions were drawn from the directions of Holy Writ — "Come, know the truth, and it shall make you free."*

These principles there laid down with so much solemnity have now the same binding force as in those revolutionary days when they were recognized and proclaimed. I am not unaware that they are old. Whatever is, is old. It is but our own poor apprehension of it that is new. It would be well if they were re-apprehended. It is not well if the great diversity of modern learning has made the truth so little of a novelty that it lacks all reverence.

The days of the Revolution were days of reverence and of applied reverence. Teaching was to a considerable extent in the hands of the clergy. Institutions of learning were presided over by clergymen. The teacher spoke with the voice of authority. He was treated with deference. He held a place in the community that was not only secure but high. The rewards of his services were comparatively large. He was a leader of the people. From him came the inspiration of liberty. It was in the meeting-houses that the Revolution was framed.

---

* John 8:32: "And ye shall know the truth, and the truth shall make you free."

This dual character little exists now, but the principle is the same. Teaching is the same high calling, but how lacking now in comparative appreciation. The compensation of many teachers and clergymen is far less than the pay of unskilled labor. The salaries of college professors are much less than like training and ability would command in the commercial world. We pay a good price to bank men to guard our money. We compensate liberally the manufacturer and the merchant; but we fail to appreciate those who guard the minds of our youth or those who preside over our congregations. We have lost our reverence for the profession of teaching and bestowed it upon the profession of acquiring.

This will have such a reaction as might be expected. Some of the clergy, seeing their own rewards are disproportionate, will draw the conclusion that all rewards are disproportionate, that the whole distribution of wealth is unsound; and turn to a belief in and an advocacy of some kind of a socialistic state. Some of our teachers, out of a like discontent, will listen too willingly to revolutionary doctrines which have not originated in meeting-houses but are the importations of those who lack nothing but the power to destroy all that our civilization holds dear. Unless these conditions are changed, these professions will not attract to their services young men of the same comparative quality of ability and character that in the past they commanded.

In our pursuit of prosperity we have forgotten and

neglected its foundations. It is true that many of our institutions of learning are well endowed and have spacious buildings, but the plant is not enough. Many modern schoolhouses put to shame any public buildings that were erected in the Colonies. I am directing attention to the comparative position of the great mass of teachers and clergymen. They are not properly appreciated or properly paid. They have provided the foundations of our liberties. The importance of their position cannot be overestimated. They have been faithful though neglected; but a state which neglects or refuses to support any class will soon find that such class neglects and refuses to support it. The remedy lies in part with private charity, in part with government action; but it lies wholly with public opinion. Private charity must worthily support its clergymen and the faculty and instructors of our higher institutions of learning; and the Government must adequately reward the teachers in its schools. In the great bound forward which has been taken in a material way, these two noble professions, the pillars of liberty and equality, have been neglected and left behind. They must be reëstablished. They must be restored to the place of reverence they formerly held.

The profession of teaching has come down to us with a sanction of antiquity greater than all else. So far back as we can peer into human history there has stood a priesthood that has led its people intellectually and morally. Teaching is leading. The fundamental needs of

humanity do not change. They are constant. These influences so potent in the development of Massachusetts
cannot be exchanged for a leadership that is bred of the
market-place, to her advantage. We must turn our eyes
from what is to what ought to be. The men of the day of
John Adams and James Bowdoin had a vision that looked
into the heart of things. They led a revolution that swept
on to a successful conclusion. They established a nation
that has endured until its flag is the ancient among the
banners of the earth. Their counsel will not be mocked.
The men of that day almost alone in history brought a
Revolution to its objective. Not only that, they reached it
in such a condition that it there remained. The counter-
attack of disorder failed entirely to dislodge it. Their success lay entirely in the convictions they had. No nation
can reject these convictions and remain a republic. Anarchy or despotism will overwhelm it.

Massachusetts established Harvard College to be a
defender of righteous convictions, of reverence for truth
and for the heralds of truth. The purpose set forth in
the Constitution is clear and plain. It recognizes with
the clear conviction of men not thinking of themselves
that the cause of America is the cause of education, but
of education with a soul, a trained intellect but guided
ever by an enlightened conscience. We of our day need
to recognize with the same vision that when these fail,
America has failed.

XXXII

PLYMOUTH, LABOR DAY

SEPTEMBER 1, 1919

"The power to preserve America ... is with
the people themselves; not one class, but all
classes; not one occupation, but all occupations;
not one citizen, but all citizens."

*Coolidge articulates his economic philosophy in this Labor
Day address. The governor explains that economic justice
"is not quite so simple as assuming that we can take from
one class and give to another class." Coolidge lays out the
hidden losses of redistribution: those of companies and their
shareholders. His point: When business and industry prosper, the people prosper. And when they fail, the people fail.*

The laws of our country have designated the first
Monday of each September as Labor Day. It is truly
an American day, for it was here that for the first time
in history a government was founded on a recognition
of the sovereignty of the citizen which has irresistibly

led to a realization of the dignity of his occupation. It is with added propriety that this day is observed this year. For the first time in five years it comes at a time when the issue of world events makes it no longer doubtful whether the American conception of work as the crowning glory of men free and equal is to prevail over the age-old European conception that work is the badge of the menial and the inferior. The American ideal has prevailed on European battle-fields through the loyalty, devotion, and sacrifice of American labor. The duty of citizenship in this hour is to strive to maintain and extend that ideal at home.

The past five years have been a time of rapid change and great progress for the American people. Not only have the hours and conditions of labor been greatly improved,* but wages have increased about one hundred

---

* Massachusetts had emerged as a leader in labor reforms over the preceding decade. In 1911, it became the second state to pass a workers' compensation law. The next year, as a state senator, Coolidge chaired a special committee that helped settle the Bread and Roses Strike. That walkout, led by the radical labor union the International Workers of the World, drew national attention to the conditions in Lawrence's textile mills. Coolidge performed well in the role and "gained the respect of both labor and capital," biographer Claude Fuess reported. But a letter Coolidge wrote to his stepmother revealed his private sentiments: "The leaders [of the strike] are socialists and anarchists, and they do not want anybody to work for wages. The trouble is not about the amount of wages; it is a small attempt to destroy all authority whether of any church or government." The sides did settle, however. The workers received a 15 percent pay raise and an increase in overtime compensation, among other improvements. Other mills and factories soon awarded similar raises. Later, as governor, Coolidge signed a law that limited the workweek for women to forty-eight

per cent. There has been a great economic change for the better among all wage-earners.

We have known that political power was with the people, because they have the votes. We have generally supposed that economic power was not with the people, because they did not own the property. This supposition, probably never true, is growing more and more to be contrary to the facts. The great outstanding fact in the economic life of America is that the wealth of the Nation is owned by the people of the Nation. The stockholders of the great corporations run into the hundreds of thousands, the small tradesmen, the thrifty householders, the tillers of the soil, the depositors in savings banks, and the now owners of government bonds, make a number that includes nearly our entire people. This would be illustrated by a few Massachusetts examples from figures which were reported in 1918:

Number of Stockholders

Railroads	40,485
Street railways	17,527
Telephone	49,688
Western Union Telegraph	9,360
	117,060

---

hours. At the federal level, Congress in 1916 passed the Keating-Owen Act, which restricted child labor, and the Adamson Act, which established an eight-hour workday for interstate railroad workers. The Supreme Court later ruled Keating-Owen unconstitutional, but it upheld the eight-hour workday.

Number of Employees

Railroads	20,604
Street railways	25,000
Telephone	11,471
Western Union Telegraph	2,065
	59,140

Savings bank depositors	2,491,646
Railroad, street railway, and telephone bonds held by savings banks and savings departments of trust companies	$267,795,636
Savings bank deposits	$1,022,342,583

Money is pouring into savings banks at the rate of $275,000 each working day.

Comment on these figures is unnecessary. There is, of course, some reduplication, but in these four public service enterprises there are in Massachusetts almost twice as many direct owners as there are employees. Two persons out of three have money in the savings bank — men, women, and children. There is this additional fact: more than one quarter of the stupendous sum of over a billion dollars of the savings of nearly two and a half million savings depositors is invested in railroad, street railway, and telephone securities.

With these examples in mind it would appear that

our problem of economic justice in Massachusetts, where we live and for which alone we can legislate, is not quite so simple as assuming that we can take from one class and give to another class. We are reaching and maintaining the position in this Commonwealth where the property class and the employed class are not separate, but identical. There is a relationship of interdependence which makes their interests the same in the long run. Most of us earn our livelihood through some form of employment. More and more of our people are in possession of some part of the wages of yesterday, and so are investors. This is the ideal economic condition.

The great aim of our Government is to protect the weak — to aid them to become strong. Massachusetts is an industrial State. If her people prosper, it must be by that means in some of its broad avenues. How can our people be made strong? Only as they draw their strength from our industries. How can they do that? Only by building up our industries and making them strong. This is fundamental. It is the place to begin. These are the instruments of all our achievement. When they fail, all fails. When they prosper, all prosper. Workmen's compensation, hours and conditions of labor are cold consolations, if there be no employment. And employment can be had only if some one finds it profitable. The greater the profit, the greater the wages.

This is one of the economic lessons of the war. It should be remembered now when taxes are to be laid, and in the period of readjustment. Taxes must be measured by the ability to meet them out of surplus income. Industry must expand or fail. It must show a surplus after all payments of wages, taxes, and returns to investors. Conscription can call once, then all is over. Just requirements can be met again and again with ever-increasing ability.

Justice and the general welfare go hand in hand. Government had to take over our transportation interests in order to do such justice to them that they could pay their employees and carry our merchandise.* They have been so restricted lest they do harm that they became unable to do good. Their surplus was gone, and we New Englanders had to go without coal. Seeing now more clearly than before the true interests of wage-earner, investor, and the public, which is the consumer, we shall hereafter be willing to pay the price and secure the benefits of justice to all these coordinate interests.

We have met the economic problem of the returning service men. They have been assimilated into our industrial life with little delay and with no disturbance of existing conditions. The day of adversity has passed. The American people met and overcame it. The day of prosperity has come. The great question now is whether the American people can endure their prosperity. I

---

* Coolidge here appears to refer to President Woodrow Wilson's December 1917 nationalization of railroads. Congress would return the railroads to private hands with the Transportation Act of 1920.

believe they can. The power to preserve America is in the same hands to-day that it was when the German army was almost at the gates of Paris. That power is with the people themselves; not one class, but all classes; not one occupation, but all occupations; not one citizen, but all citizens.

During the past five years we have heard many false prophets. Some were honest, but unwise; some plain slackers; a very few were simply public enemies. Had their counsels prevailed, America would have been destroyed. In general they appealed to the lower impulses of the people, for in their ignorance they believed the most powerful motive of this Nation was a sodden self-ishness. They said the war would never affect us; we should confine ourselves to making money. They argued for peace at any price. They opposed selective service. They sought to prevent sending soldiers to Europe. They advocated peace by negotiation. They were answered from beginning to end by the loyalty of the American workingmen and the wisdom of their leaders. That loy-alty and that wisdom will not desert us now. The voices that would have lured us to destruction were unheeded. All counsels of selfishness were unheeded, and America responded with a spirit which united our people as never before to the call of duty.

Having accomplished this great task, having emerged from the war the strongest, the least burdened nation on earth, are we now to fail before our lesser task? Are we

to turn aside from the path that has led us to success?
Who now will set selfishness above duty? The counsel
that Samuel Gompers* gave is still sound, when he said
in effect, "America may not be perfect. It has the imper-
fections of all things human. But it is the best country
on earth, and the man who will not work for it, who will
not fight for it, and if need be die for it, is unworthy to
live in it."

Happily, the day when the call to fight or die is now
past. But the day when it is the duty of all Americans
to work will remain forever. Our great need now is for
more of everything for everybody. It is not money that
the nation or the world needs to-day, but the products
of labor. These products are to be secured only by the
united efforts of an entire people. The trained business
man and the humblest workman must each contribute.
All of us must work, and in that work there should be
no interruption. There must be more food, more cloth-
ing, more shelter. The directors of industry must direct
it more efficiently, the workers in industry must work
in it more efficiently. Such a course saved us in war;
only such a course can preserve us in peace. The power

---

* Samuel Gompers founded the American Federation of Labor and served
as its president for decades. Less than two weeks after this speech, Governor Coolidge would send the labor leader the telegram that made Coolidge
a national figure. At the height of the Boston police strike, Coolidge told
Gompers, "There is no right to strike against the public safety by anybody,
anywhere, any time." (See page 213.)

to preserve America, with all that it now means to the world, all the great hope that it holds for humanity, lies in the hands of the people. Talents and opportunity exist. Application only is uncertain. May Labor Day of 1919 declare with an increased emphasis the resolution of all Americans to work for America.

XXXIII

WESTFIELD

SEPTEMBER 3, 1919

"The great promise of the future lies in
the loyalty and devotion of the people
to their own Government."

*In the summer of 1919, restless cities across the country were
enduring rioting and vandalism. In Boston, the police force
was threatening to walk off the job, an event which meant that
not only the mayor but also Governor Coolidge would need
to keep peace. Coolidge seized the occasion of the 250th anniversary of the town of Westfield, Massachusetts, to remind
Americans of their tradition of law and order. He praised
the town for erecting a statue to its own William Shepard,
who in 1787 had led the Massachusetts militia that defended
the Springfield Armory during Shays's Rebellion. He also
reminded listeners of Jonathan Smith of Lanesborough, a
farmer who in the same era stood up for the Constitution
and against petty class envy. In troubled times, Coolidge*

*admonished, we must respect the "duly constituted authority
of the people."*

W e come here on this occasion to honor the past,
and in that honor render more secure the present. It was by such men as settled Westfield, and two
hundred and fifty years ago established by law a char-
tered and ordered government, that the foundations
of Massachusetts were laid. And it was on the foundations of Massachusetts that there began that training of
the people for the great days that were to come, when
they were prepared to endorse and support the principles set out in the Declaration of Independence, the
Constitution of the United States of America, and the
Emancipation Proclamation of Abraham Lincoln. Here
were planted the same seeds of righteousness victorious
which later flourished with such abundance at Saratoga,
at Gettysburg, and at the second battle of the Marne.
Stupendous results, the product of a people working with
an everlasting purpose.

While celebrating the history of Westfield, this day
has been set apart to the memory of one of her most
illustrious sons, General William Shepard.* To others are
assigned the history of your town and the biography of
your soldier. Into those particulars I shall not enter. But
the principles of government and of citizenship which

---

* The statue of Shepard still stands in Westfield today.

they so well represent, and nobly illustrate, will never be untimely or unworthy of reiteration.

The political history of Westfield has seen the success of a great forward movement, to which it contributed its part, in establishing the principle, that the individual in his rights is supreme, and that "governments derive their just powers from the consent of the governed."* It is the establishment of liberty, under an ordered form of government, in this ancient town, by the people themselves, that to-day draws us here in admiration of her achievements. When we turn to the life of her patriot son we see that he no less grandly illustrated the principle, that to such government, so established, the people owe an allegiance which has the binding power of the most solemn obligation.

There is such a disposition in these days to deny that our Government was formed by, or is now in control of, the people, that a glance at the history of the days of General Shepard is peculiarly pertinent and instructive.

The Constitution of Massachusetts, with its noble Declaration of Rights, was adopted in 1780. Under it we still live with scarce any changes that affect the rights of the people. The end of the Revolutionary War was 1783. Shays's Rebellion was in 1787.† The American Constitution

---

* The Declaration of Independence famously says, "Governments are instituted among Men, deriving their just powers from the consent of the governed."

† Daniel Shays, a farmer and Revolutionary War veteran, mounted an armed uprising in western Massachusetts to oppose high taxes and difficult economic

was ratified and adopted in 1788. These dates tell us what the form of government was in this period.

If there are any who doubt that our institutions, formed in those days, did not establish a peoples' government, let them study the action of the Massachusetts Convention which ratified the Federal Constitution in 1788. Presiding over it was the popular patriot Governor John Hancock. On the floor sat Samuel Adams, who had been the father of the Revolution, preëminent champion of the liberty of the people. Such an influence had he, that his assertion of satisfaction, was enough to carry the delegates. Like a majority of the members he came opposed to ratification. Having totally thrown off the authority of foreign power, they came suspicious of all outside authority. Besides there were eighteen members who had taken part in Shays's Rebellion, so hostile were they to the execution of all law. Mr. Adams was finally convinced by a gathering of the workingmen among his constituents, who exercised their constitutional right of instructing their representatives. Their opinion was presented to him by Paul Revere. "How many mechanics were at the Green Dragon* when these resolutions were passed?" asked Mr. Adams. "More, sir, than the Green

---

conditions. The central government's struggle to put down the rebellion highlighted that government's weaknesses under the Articles of Confederation.

    * Boston's Green Dragon tavern hosted meetings of Revere's Sons of Liberty. Historians have referred to the Green Dragon as the "headquarters of the Revolution."

Dragon could hold." "And where were the rest?" "In the streets, sir." "And how many were in the streets?" "More than there are stars in the sky." This is supposed to have convinced the great Massachusetts tribune that it was his duty to support ratification.

There were those, however, who distrusted the Constitution and distrusted its proponents. They viewed lawyers and men of means with great jealousy. Amos Singletary* expressed their sentiments in the form of an argument that has not ceased to be repeated in the discussion of all public affairs. "These lawyers," said he, "and men of learning and moneyed men that talk so finely and gloss over matters so smoothly, to make us poor illiterates swallow the pill, expect to get into Congress themselves. They mean to be managers of the Constitution. They mean to get all the money into their hands and then they will swallow up us little folk, like the great Leviathan, Mr. President: yes, just like the whale swallowed up Jonah." In the convention sat Jonathan Smith, a farmer from Lanesboro. He had seen Shays's Rebellion in Berkshire.† There had been no better example of a man of the people desiring the common good.

---

* The Anti-Federalist Singletary, a former state senator, spoke out against the Constitution at the Massachusetts ratifying convention.

† The town of Lanesborough sits in Massachusetts's Berkshire County, from which many of Shays's rebels came. In the speech Coolidge quotes below, farmer Jonathan Smith referred to Shays's Rebellion when he spoke of "anarchy."

"I am a plain man," said Mr. Smith, "and am not used
to speak in public, but I am going to show the effects of
anarchy, that you may see why I wish for good government. Last winter people took up arms, and then, if you
went to speak to them, you had the musket of death presented to your breast. They would rob you of your property, threaten to burn your houses, oblige you to be on
your guard night and day. Alarms spread from town to
town, families were broken up; the tender mother would
cry, 'Oh, my son is among them! What shall I do for my
child?' Some were taken captive; children taken out of
their schools and carried away.... How dreadful was this!
Our distress was so great that we should have been glad
to snatch at anything that looked like a government....
Now, Mr. President, when I saw this Constitution, I
found that it was a cure for these disorders. I got a copy
of it, and read it over and over.... I did not go to any
lawyer, to ask his opinion; we have no lawyer in our
town, and we do well enough without. My honourable
old daddy there (pointing to Mr. Singletary) won't think
that I expect to be a Congressman, and swallow up the
liberties of the people. I never had any post, nor do I
want one. But I don't think the worse of the Constitution because lawyers, and men of learning, and moneyed
men are fond of it. I am not of such a jealous make.
They that are honest men themselves are not apt to sus-
pect other people.... Brother farmers, let us suppose a
case, now. Suppose you had a farm of 50 acres, and your

title was disputed, and there was a farm of 5000 acres joined to you that belonged to a man of learning, and his title was involved in the same difficulty; would you not be glad to have him for your friend, rather than to stand alone in the dispute? Well, the case is the same. These lawyers, these moneyed men, these men of learning, are all embarked in the same cause with us, and we must all sink or swim together. Shall we throw the Constitution overboard because it does not please us all alike? Suppose two or three of you had been at the pains to break up a piece of rough land and sow it with wheat: would you let it lie waste because you could not agree what sort of a fence to make? Would it not be better to put up a fence that did not please every one's fancy, rather than keep disputing about it until the wild beasts came in and devoured the crop? Some gentlemen say, Don't be in a hurry; take time to consider. I say, There is a time to sow and a time to reap. We sowed our seed when we sent men to the Federal Convention, now is the time to reap the fruit of our labour; and if we do not do it now, I am afraid we shall never have another opportunity."

There spoke the common sense of the common man of the Commonwealth. The counsel of the farmer from the country, joined with the resolutions of the working-men from the city, carried the convention and the Constitution was ratified. In the light of succeeding history, who shall say, that it was not the voice of the people, speaking with the voice of Infinite Authority?

The attitude of Samuel Adams, William Shepard, Jonathan Smith and the workingmen of Boston toward government, is worthy of our constant emulation. They had not hesitated to take up arms against tyranny in the Revolution, but having established a government of the people they were equally determined to defend and support it. They hated the usurper whether king, or Parliament, or mob, but they bowed before the duly constituted authority of the people.

When the question of pardoning the convicted leaders of the rebellion came up, Adams opposed it. "In monarchies," he said, "the crime of treason and rebellion may admit of being pardoned or lightly punished; but the man who dares to rebel against the laws of a republic ought to suffer death." We are all glad mercy prevailed and pardon was granted. But the calm judgment of Samuel Adams, the lover of liberty, "the man of the town meeting" whose clear vision, taught by bitter experience, saw that all usurpation is tyranny, must not go unheeded now. The authority of a just government derived from the consent of the governed, has back of it a Power that does not fail.

All wars bring in their trail great hardships. They existed in the day of General Shepard. They exist now. Having set up a sound government in Massachusetts, having secured their independence, as the result of a victorious war, the people expected a season of easy prosperity. In that they were temporarily disappointed. Some rebelling, were overthrown. The adoption of the Federal Constitution brought relief and prosperity.

Success has attended the establishment here of a government of the people. We of this day have just finished a victorious war that has added new glory to American arms. We are facing some hardships, but they are not serious. Private obligations are not so large as to be burdensome. Taxes can be paid. Prosperity abounds. But the great promise of the future lies in the loyalty and devotion of the people to their own Government. They are firm in the conviction of the fathers, that liberty is increased only by increasing the determination to support a government of the people, as established in this ancient town, and defended by its patriotic sons.

The Commonwealth of Massachusetts
By His Excellency Calvin Coolidge, Governor

A PROCLAMATION

"I call on every citizen to aid me in the
maintenance of law and order."

On September 9, 1919, more than a thousand Boston police officers — the majority of the force — went on strike. Rioting and looting broke out across the city. By September 11, six people were dead and as many as a hundred were wounded. With fears that a general strike would follow, Coolidge faced pressure to compromise with the police union. Political advisers also warned that failing to settle would cost him his reelection. But the governor held firm, issuing this proclamation.

The entire State Guard of Massachusetts has been called out. Under the Constitution the Governor is the Commander-in-Chief thereof by an authority of which he could not if he chose divest himself. That command I must and will exercise. Under the law I hereby call on all the police of Boston who have loyally and in a never-to-be-forgotten way remained on duty to aid me in the performance of my duty of the restoration and maintenance of order in the city of Boston, and each of such officers is required to act in obedience to such orders as I may hereafter issue or cause to be issued.

I call on every citizen to aid me in the maintenance of law and order.

Given at the Executive Chamber, in Boston, this eleventh day of September, in the year of our Lord one thousand nine hundred and nineteen, and of the Independence of the United States of America the one hundred and forty-fourth.

By His Excellency the Governor,   CALVIN COOLIDGE

ALBERT P. LANGTRY,
Secretary of the Commonwealth.

God save the Commonwealth of Massachusetts.

AN ORDER

"You are hereby directed...to proceed in the
performance of your duties as Police Commissioner
of the city of Boston under my command."

*The Boston police reported to the commissioner, who reported
to the governor. But Boston mayor Andrew Peters determined that the law allowed him to take over the police force.
Peters announced that he was doing so, effectively ousting
Police Commissioner Edwin Curtis. In response, Coolidge
studied Massachusetts law and discovered a statute that
gave the governor authority over the city's police. With this
executive order, Coolidge exercised that authority.*

BOSTON, *September* 11, 1919

To Edwin U. Curtis: As you are Police Commissioner
of the City of Boston,

Executive Order No. 1

You are hereby directed, for the purpose of assisting me in the performance of my duty, pursuant to the proclamation issued by me this day, to proceed in the performance of your duties as Police Commissioner of the city of Boston under my command and in obedience to such orders as I shall issue from time to time, and obey only such orders as I may so issue or transmit.

CALVIN COOLIDGE
Governor of Massachusetts

A TELEGRAM

"There is no right to strike against the public
safety by anybody, anywhere, any time."

This terse message catapulted Coolidge to national promi-
nence. On Saturday, September 13, Police Commissioner
Edwin Curtis, with Coolidge's support, officially discharged
the striking policemen. Late that night, American Federa-
tion of Labor president Samuel Gompers sent Governor
Coolidge a telegram, condemning Curtis's "autocratic and
unwarranted position." The next day, Coolidge sent this
blunt response.

The governor's telegram made the front pages of news-
papers across the country. Coolidge's publisher scrambled to
add the now-famous telegram to this book, which reached
readers' hands less than a month later.

BOSTON, MASS., *Sept.* 14, 1919

MR. SAMUEL GOMPERS
President, American Federation of Labor, New York City, N.Y.

Replying to your telegram, I have already refused to remove the Police Commissioner of Boston. I did not appoint him. He can assume no position which the courts would uphold except what the people have by the authority of their law vested in him. He speaks only with their voice. The right of the police of Boston to affiliate has always been questioned, never granted, is now prohibited.* The suggestion of President Wilson to Washington does not apply to Boston.† There the police have remained on duty. Here the Policemen's Union left their duty, an action which President Wilson characterized as a crime against civilization.‡ Your assertion

---

* Here Coolidge directly refutes Gompers's contention that the police's right to affiliate with a labor union "has been denied, a right which has heretofore never been questioned."

† The police force in Washington, D.C., had also affiliated with the American Federation of Labor. President Woodrow Wilson's private secretary issued this vague statement on the matter: "The president suggests the great advisability of postponing any issue regarding the police situation until the forthcoming industrial conference at Washington," scheduled to begin October 6. Wilson's advice probably pleased the Washington police, because it suggested they might have a few more weeks to showcase their troubles.

‡ The labor leader Gompers apparently misread President Wilson. In the president, Coolidge found a strong supporter. Once President Wilson heard about the rioting in Boston, he said that "a strike of the policemen of a great city, leaving that city at the mercy of an army of thugs, is a crime against civi-

that the Commissioner was wrong cannot justify the wrong of leaving the city unguarded. That furnished the opportunity, the criminal element furnished the action. There is no right to strike against the public safety by anybody, anywhere, any time. You ask that the public safety again be placed in the hands of these same policemen while they continue in disobedience to the laws of Massachusetts and in their refusal to obey the orders of the Police Department. Nineteen men have been tried and removed. Others having abandoned their duty, their places have, under the law, been declared vacant on the opinion of the Attorney-General. I can suggest no authority outside the courts to take further action. I wish to join and assist in taking a broad view of every situation. A grave responsibility rests on all of us. You can depend on me to support you in every legal action and sound policy. I am equally determined to defend the sovereignty of Massachusetts and to maintain the authority and jurisdiction over her public officers where it has been placed by the Constitution and law of her people.

CALVIN COOLIDGE
Governor of Massachusetts

---

lization." Wilson also sent a telegram to the commissioners of the District of Columbia, saying, "I think that any association of the police force of the Capital City, or of any great city, whose object is to bring pressure upon the public or the community such as will endanger the public peace or embarrass the maintenance of order, should in no case be countenanced or permitted."

ACKNOWLEDGMENTS

⁓

In editing a new edition of *Have Faith in Massachusetts*, we placed our faith in the Bay State. Massachusetts did not let us down. We owe a debt to Julie Bartlett Nelson and her colleagues at the Forbes Library in Northampton, which will be honoring the centennial of the president's service with a new digital exhibition of photographs of Coolidge from its collection. In addition, the Leslie Jones Collection of the Boston Public Library graciously shared some of Jones's stellar photography for this volume; we are grateful to the Boston Public Library and Leslie Jones's descendant Bob Cullum for several fine images of the Coolidges. The Lawrence History Center supplied a photograph of the Bread and

Roses Strike. The Millicent Library in Fairhaven offered their scan of Manjirō's image.

Friends from other parts of Coolidge's home region, New England, likewise did much to support this edition. We thank Christopher Coolidge Jeter, Jennifer Coolidge Harville, and John Sayles for their support for this new edition. The Vermont Historical Society supplied some images as well; yet more of those items will be featured in a Coolidge Foundation online exhibit in 2023. A trove of documents was recently digitized by the Library of Congress in Washington; we thank the Library of Congress and the National Archives for the images they provided.

The Foundation thanks production supervisor Jed Donahue, who with this book marks his second project with the Coolidge Foundation. We are grateful to Coolidge publications associate William Pettinger, whose research improved this work. Finally, the Foundation owes a tremendous debt to the book's guest editor and our Foundation vice chair, James Douglas. Like Coolidge, Jim made his career in politics, including giving four terms to Vermont as the state's governor. Jim's editorial insights and his tremendous leadership have elevated the quality of not only the book in your hands but also much of the Foundation's work.

Amity Shlaes and Matthew Denhart
Series Editors

INDEX

ABOUT THE COOLIDGE FOUNDATION

The Calvin Coolidge Presidential Foundation is the official foundation dedicated to preserving the legacy and advancing the values of America's thirtieth president. In the absence of an official, federally funded presidential library, the Coolidge Foundation was formed in 1960 by John Coolidge, the president's son, along with a group of fellow Coolidge enthusiasts. The Foundation is based at the president's birthplace in Plymouth Notch, Vermont. There it joins its longtime partner, the state of Vermont, in hosting visitors throughout the summer season. At Coolidge House in Washington, D.C., the Foundation maintains another Coolidge exhibit. Wherever it operates, the Foundation seeks to increase Americans' understanding of President Coolidge and the values he championed.

The Foundation's signature initiative is the Coolidge Scholars Program, a full-ride, four-year, merit scholarship that recipients can use at any accredited college or university in the United States. Each year thousands of high school students study President Coolidge and read his autobiography through the course of applying for the scholarship. Currently, three to four new Coolidge Scholars are selected annually, and a group of one hundred top applicants earn the distinction of "Coolidge Senator." The Foundation also operates a national high school debate program, the Coolidge Cup. From across the nation, debaters converge to compete for the Coolidge Cup on the Fourth of July, Coolidge's birthday, in Plymouth Notch. To date, more than 2,000 students have participated in Coolidge League debate.

We invite you to join our work in sharing Silent Cal with the nation. For more information about how to get involved, please visit us online at **CoolidgeFoundation.org**.